interchange
FIFTH EDITION

3A

Student's Book

Jack C. Richards
with Jonathan Hull and Susan Proctor

WITH ONLINE SELF-STUDY

CAMBRIDGE UNIVERSITY PRESS

CAMBRIDGE
UNIVERSITY PRESS

University Printing House, Cambridge CB2 8BS, United Kingdom

One Liberty Plaza, 20th Floor, New York, NY 10006, USA

477 Williamstown Road, Port Melbourne, VIC 3207, Australia

4843/24, 2nd Floor, Ansari Road, Daryaganj, Delhi – 110002, India

79 Anson Road, #06–04/06, Singapore 079906

Cambridge University Press is part of the University of Cambridge.

It furthers the University's mission by disseminating knowledge in the pursuit of education, learning and research at the highest international levels of excellence.

www.cambridge.org
Information on this title: www.cambridge.org/9781316624074

© Cambridge University Press 2005, 2017

This publication is in copyright. Subject to statutory exception and to the provisions of relevant collective licensing agreements, no reproduction of any part may take place without the written permission of Cambridge University Press.

First published 2005
Second edition 2013
20　19　18　17　16　15　14　13　12　11　10　9　8　7　6　5　4　3　2　1

Printed in Malaysia by Vivar Printing

A catalogue record for this publication is available from the British Library

ISBN	9781316620519	Student's Book 3 with Online Self-Study
ISBN	9781316620533	Student's Book 3A with Online Self-Study
ISBN	9781316620540	Student's Book 3B with Online Self-Study
ISBN	9781316620557	Student's Book 3 with Online Self-Study and Online Workbook
ISBN	9781316620564	Student's Book 3A with Online Self-Study and Online Workbook
ISBN	9781316620588	Student's Book 3B with Online Self-Study and Online Workbook
ISBN	9781316622766	Workbook 3
ISBN	9781316622773	Workbook 3A
ISBN	9781316622797	Workbook 3B
ISBN	9781316622803	Teacher's Edition 3 with Complete Assessment Program
ISBN	9781316622308	Class Audio CDs 3
ISBN	9781316624050	Full Contact 3 with Online Self-Study
ISBN	9781316624074	Full Contact 3A with Online Self-Study
ISBN	9781316624098	Full Contact 3B with Online Self-Study
ISBN	9781316622322	Presentation Plus 3

Additional resources for this publication at www.cambridge.org/interchange

Cambridge University Press has no responsibility for the persistence or accuracy of URLs for external or third-party internet websites referred to in this publication, and does not guarantee that any content on such websites is, or will remain, accurate or appropriate. Information regarding prices, travel timetables, and other factual information given in this work is correct at the time of first printing but Cambridge University Press does not guarantee the accuracy of such information thereafter.

Informed by teachers

Teachers from all over the world helped develop *Interchange Fifth Edition*. They looked at everything – from the color of the designs to the topics in the conversations – in order to make sure that this course will work in the classroom. We heard from 1,500 teachers in:

- Surveys
- Focus Groups
- In-Depth Reviews

We appreciate the help and input from everyone. In particular, we'd like to give the following people our special thanks:

Jader Franceschi, **Actúa Idiomas,** Bento Gonçalves, Rio Grande do Sul, Brazil

Juliana Dos Santos Voltan Costa, **Actus Idiomas,** São Paulo, Brazil

Ella Osorio, **Angelo State University,** San Angelo, TX, US

Mary Hunter, **Angelo State University,** San Angelo, TX, US

Mario César González, **Angloamericano de Monterrey, SC,** Monterrey, Mexico

Samantha Shipman, **Auburn High School,** Auburn, AL, US

Linda, **Bernick Language School,** Radford, VA, US

Dave Lowrance, **Bethesda University of California,** Yorba Linda, CA, US

Tajbakhsh Hosseini, **Bezmialem Vakif University,** Istanbul, Turkey

Dilek Gercek, **Bil English,** Izmir, Turkey

Erkan Kolat, **Biruni University, ELT,** Istanbul, Turkey

Nika Gutkowska, **Bluedata International,** New York, NY, US

Daniel Alcocer Gómez, **Cecati 92,** Guadalupe, Nuevo León, Mexico

Samantha Webb, **Central Middle School,** Milton-Freewater, OR, US

Verónica Salgado, **Centro Anglo Americano,** Cuernavaca, Mexico

Ana Rivadeneira Martínez and Georgia P. de Machuca, **Centro de Educación Continua – Universidad Politécnica del Ecuador,** Quito, Ecuador

Anderson Francisco Guimerães Maia, **Centro Cultural Brasil Estados Unidos,** Belém, Brazil

Rosana Mariano, **Centro Paula Souza,** São Paulo, Brazil

Carlos de la Paz Arroyo, Teresa Noemí Parra Alarcón, Gilberto Bastida Gaytan, Manuel Esquivel Román, and Rosa Cepeda Tapia, **Centro Universitario Angloamericano,** Cuernavaca, Morelos, Mexico

Antonio Almeida, **CETEC,** Morelos, Mexico

Cinthia Ferreira, **Cinthia Ferreira Languages Services,** Toronto, ON, Canada

Phil Thomas and Sérgio Sanchez, **CLS Canadian Language School,** São Paulo, Brazil

Celia Concannon, **Cochise College,** Nogales, AZ, US

Maria do Carmo Rocha and CAOP English team, **Colégio Arquidiocesano Ouro Preto – Unidade Cônego Paulo Dilascio,** Ouro Preto, Brazil

Kim Rodriguez, **College of Charleston North,** Charleston, SC, US

Jesús Leza Alvarado, **Coparmex English Institute,** Monterrey, Mexico

John Partain, **Cortazar,** Guanajuato, Mexico

Alexander Palencia Navas, **Cursos de Lenguas, Universidad del Atlántico,** Barranquilla, Colombia

Kenneth Johan Gerardo Steenhuisen Cera, Melfi Osvaldo Guzman Triana, and Carlos Alberto Algarín Jiminez, **Cursos de Lenguas Extranjeras Universidad del Atlantico,** Barranquilla, Colombia

Jane P Kerford, **East Los Angeles College,** Pasadena, CA, US

Daniela, **East Village,** Campinas, São Paulo, Brazil

Rosalva Camacho Orduño, **Easy English for Groups S.A. de C.V.,** Monterrey, Nuevo León, Mexico

Adonis Gimenez Fusetti, **Easy Way Idiomas,** Ibiúna, Brazil

Eileen Thompson, **Edison Community College,** Piqua, OH, US

Ahminne Handeri O.L Froede, **Englishouse escola de idiomas,** Teófilo Otoni, Brazil

Ana Luz Delgado-Izazola, **Escuela Nacional Preparatoria 5, UNAM,** Mexico City, Mexico

Nancy Alarcón Mendoza, **Facultad de Estudios Superiores Zaragoza, UNAM,** Mexico City, Mexico

Marcilio N. Barros, **Fast English USA,** Campinas, São Paulo, Brazil

Greta Douthat, **FCI Ashland,** Ashland, KY, US

Carlos Lizárraga González, **Grupo Educativo Anglo Americano, S.C.,** Mexico City, Mexico

Hugo Fernando Alcántar Valle, **Instituto Politécnico Nacional, Escuela Superior de Comercio y Administración-Unidad Santotomás, Celex Esca Santo Tomás,** Mexico City, Mexico

Sueli Nascimento, **Instituto Superior de Educação do Rio de Janeiro,** Rio de Janeiro, Brazil

Elsa F Monteverde, **International Academic Services,** Miami, FL, US

Laura Anand, **Irvine Adult School,** Irvine, CA, US

Prof. Marli T. Fernandes (principal) and Prof. Dr. Jefferson J. Fernandes (pedagogue), **Jefferson Idiomas,** São Paulo, Brazil

Herman Bartelen, **Kanda Gaigo Gakuin,** Tokyo, Japan

Cassia Silva, **Key Languages,** Key Biscayne, FL, US

Sister Mary Hope, **Kyoto Notre Dame Joshi Gakuin,** Kyoto, Japan

Nate Freedman, **LAL Language Centres,** Boston, MA, US

Richard Janzen, **Langley Secondary School,** Abbotsford, BC, Canada

Christina Abel Gabardo, **Language House,** Campo Largo, Brazil

Ivonne Castro, **Learn English International,** Cali, Colombia

Julio Cesar Maciel Rodrigues, **Liberty Centro de Línguas,** São Paulo, Brazil

Ann Gibson, **Maynard High School,** Maynard, MA, US

Martin Darling, **Meiji Gakuin Daigaku,** Tokyo, Japan

Dax Thomas, **Meiji Gakuin Daigaku,** Yokohama, Kanagawa, Japan

Derya Budak, **Mevlana University,** Konya, Turkey

B Sullivan, **Miami Valley Career Technical Center International Program,** Dayton, OH, US

Julio Velazquez, **Milo Language Center,** Weston, FL, US

Daiane Siqueira da Silva, Luiz Carlos Buontempo, Marlete Avelina de Oliveira Cunha, Marcos Paulo Segatti, Morgana Eveline de Oliveira, Nadia Lia Gino Alo, and Paul Hyde Budgen, **New Interchange-Escola de Idiomas,** São Paulo, Brazil

Patrícia França Furtado da Costa, Juiz de Fora, Brazil Patricia Servín

Chris Pollard, **North West Regional College SK,** North Battleford, SK, Canada

Olga Amy, **Notre Dame High School,** Red Deer, Canada

Amy Garrett, **Ouachita Baptist University,** Arkadelphia, AR, US

Mervin Curry, **Palm Beach State College,** Boca Raton, FL, US

Julie Barros, **Quality English Studio,** Guarulhos, São Paulo, Brazil

Teodoro González Saldaña and Jesús Monserrrta Mata Franco, **Race Idiomas,** Mexico City, Mexico

Autumn Westphal and Noga La`or, **Rennert International,** New York, NY, US

Antonio Gallo and Javy Palau, **Rigby Idiomas,** Monterrey, Mexico Tatiane Gabriela Sperb do Nascimento, **Right Way,** Igrejinha, Brazil

Mustafa Akgül, **Selahaddin Eyyubi Universitesi,** Diyarbakır, Turkey

James Drury M. Fonseca, **Senac Idiomas Fortaleza,** Fortaleza, Ceara, Brazil

Manoel Fialho S Neto, **Senac – PE,** Recife, Brazil

Jane Imber, **Small World,** Lawrence, KS, US

Tony Torres, **South Texas College,** McAllen, TX, US

Janet Rose, **Tennessee Foreign Language Institute,** College Grove, TN, US

Todd Enslen, **Tohoku University,** Sendai, Miyagi, Japan

Daniel Murray, **Torrance Adult School,** Torrance, CA, US

Juan Manuel Pulido Mendoza, **Universidad del Atlántico,** Barranquilla, Colombia

Juan Carlos Vargas Millán, **Universidad Libre Seccional Cali,** Cali (Valle del Cauca), Colombia

Carmen Cecilia Llanos Ospina, **Universidad Libre Seccional Cali,** Cali, Colombia

Jorge Noriega Zenteno, **Universidad Politécnica del Valle de México,** Estado de México, Mexico

Aimee Natasha Holguin S., **Universidad Politécnica del Valle de México UPVM,** Tultitlàn Estado de México, Mexico

Christian Selene Bernal Barraza, **UPVM Universidad Politécnica del Valle de México,** Ecatepec, Mexico

Lizeth Ramos Acosta, **Universidad Santiago de Cali,** Cali, Colombia

Silvana Dushku, **University of Illinois Champaign,** IL, US

Deirdre McMurtry, **University of Nebraska – Omaha,** Omaha, NE, US

Jason E Mower, **University of Utah,** Salt Lake City, UT, US

Paul Chugg, **Vanguard Taylor Language Institute,** Edmonton, Alberta, Canada

Henry Mulak, **Varsity Tutors,** Los Angeles, CA, US

Shirlei Strucker Calgaro and Hugo Guilherme Karrer, **VIP Centro de Idiomas,** Panambi, Rio Grande do Sul, Brazil

Eleanor Kelly, **Waseda Daigaku Extension Centre,** Tokyo, Japan

Sherry Ashworth, **Wichita State University,** Wichita, KS, US

Laine Bourdene, **William Carey University,** Hattiesburg, MS, US

Serap Aydın, Istanbul, Turkey

Liliana Covino, Guarulhos, Brazil

Yannuarys Jiménez, Barranquilla, Colombia

Juliana Morais Pazzini, Toronto, ON, Canada

Marlon Sanches, Montreal, Canada

Additional content contributed by Kenna Bourke, Inara Couto, Nic Harris, Greg Manin, Ashleigh Martinez, Laura McKenzie, Paul McIntyre, Clara Prado, Lynne Robertson, Mari Vargo, Theo Walker, and Maria Lucia Zaorob.

Classroom Language Student questions

Plan of Book 3A

Titles/Topics	Speaking	Grammar
UNIT 1 — PAGES 2–7 **That's my kind of friend!** Personality types and qualities; relationships; likes and dislikes	Describing personalities; expressing likes and dislikes; agreeing and disagreeing; complaining	Relative pronouns as subjects and objects; *it* clauses + adverbial clauses with *when*
UNIT 2 — PAGES 8–13 **Working 9 to 5** Jobs; career benefits; job skills; summer jobs	Talking about possible careers; describing jobs; deciding between two jobs	Gerund phrases as subjects and objects; comparisons with adjectives, nouns, verbs, and past participles

PROGRESS CHECK — PAGES 14–15

Titles/Topics	Speaking	Grammar
UNIT 3 — PAGES 16–21 **Lend a hand.** Favors; formal and informal requests; messages	Making direct and indirect requests; accepting and declining requests	Requests with modals, *if* clauses, and gerunds; indirect requests
UNIT 4 — PAGES 22–27 **What happened?** The media; news stories; exceptional events	Narrating a story; describing events and experiences in the past	Past continuous vs. simple past; past perfect

PROGRESS CHECK — PAGES 28–29

Titles/Topics	Speaking	Grammar
UNIT 5 — PAGES 30–35 **Expanding your horizons** Cultural comparisons and culture shock; moving abroad; emotions; customs; tourism and travel abroad	Talking about moving abroad; expressing emotions; describing cultural expectations; giving advice	Noun phrases containing relative clauses; expectations: *the custom to*, *(not) supposed to*, *expected to*, *(not) acceptable to*
UNIT 6 — PAGES 36–41 **That needs fixing.** Consumer complaints; everyday problems; problems with electronics; repairs	Describing problems; making complaints; explaining something that needs to be done	Describing problems with past participles as adjectives and with nouns; describing problems with *need* + gerund, *need* + passive infinitive, and *keep* + gerund

PROGRESS CHECK — PAGES 42–43

Titles/Topics	Speaking	Grammar
UNIT 7 — PAGES 44–49 **What can we do?** The environment; global challenges; current issues	Identifying and describing problems; coming up with solutions	Passive in the present continuous and present perfect; prepositions of cause; infinitive clauses and phrases
UNIT 8 — PAGES 50–55 **Never stop learning.** Education; learner choices; strategies for learning; life skills	Asking about preferences; discussing different skills to be learned; talking about learning methods; talking about life skills	*Would rather* and *would prefer*; *by* + gerund to describe how to do things

PROGRESS CHECK — PAGES 56–57

GRAMMAR PLUS — PAGES 132–149

Pronunciation/Listening	Writing/Reading	Interchange Activity
Linked sounds Listening for descriptions of people; listening for opinions	Writing a description of a good friend "Social Networks That Aren't for Everyone": Reading about unusual social networking sites	"Personality quiz": Interviewing a classmate to find out about personality characteristics PAGE 114
Stress with compound nouns Listening to the good and bad parts of a job; listening for complaints	Writing about two career choices "The Perfect Workplace?": Reading about different types of workplaces	"Networking": Comparing people's careers and personalities to make a seating chart for a dinner party PAGE 115
Unreleased consonants Listening to people making, accepting, and declining requests	Writing a message with requests "Can You Tell It Like It Is?": Reading about talking to friends about difficult topics	"Beg and borrow": Asking classmates to borrow items; lending or refusing to lend items PAGE 116
Intonation in complex sentences Listening to news stories; listening to messages and a podcast	Writing a personal account "Believing More Than We Should": Reading about the reliability of online content	"Spin a yarn": Inventing a story from three random elements PAGE 117
Word stress in sentences Listening for information about living abroad; listening to opinions about customs	Writing a pamphlet for tourists "Culture Shock": Reading about moving to another country	"Cultural dos and taboos": Comparing customs in different countries PAGE 118
Contrastive stress Listening to complaints; listening to people exchange things in a store; listening to a conversation about a "throwaway culture"	Writing a critical online review "Ask the Fixer!": Reading about a problem with a ride-sharing service	"Home makeover": Comparing problems in two pictures of an apartment PAGES 119, 120
Reduction of auxiliary verbs Listening to environmental problems; listening for solutions	Writing a post on a community website "Turning an Invasion Into an Advantage": Reading about a creative solution to lionfish on St. Lucia	"Take action!": Choosing an issue and deciding on an effective method of protest; devising a strategy PAGE 121
Intonation in questions of choice Listening to a conversation with a guidance counselor; listening for additional information	Writing about a skill "Are You Studying the 'Right' Way?": Reading about different studying styles	"Making choices": Choosing between different things you want to learn PAGE 122

1 That's my kind of friend!

▸ Discuss personalities and qualities
▸ Discuss likes and dislikes

1 SNAPSHOT

ROMANCE AND MARRIAGE IN THE UNITED STATES

When choosing a spouse or partner, single Americans want to find someone with . . .

■ men ■ women

Quality	Men	Women
Similar ideas about having and raising children	62%	70%
A steady job	46%	78%
The same beliefs	31%	38%
At least as much education	28%	28%
The same background	7%	10%

In your opinion, which of the things above are most important to look for in a partner? Did any of the items surprise you? Which? Why?
Are there other important qualities missing from the list?

2 CONVERSATION What *are* you looking for?

A Listen and practice.

Joe: What are you doing?
Roy: I'm setting up my profile for this online dating site. I have to describe the kind of person I'm looking for.
Joe: I see. And what are you looking for?
Roy: Oh, I like people who aren't too serious and who have a good sense of humor. You know, someone I can have fun with.
Joe: OK. Uh, what else?
Roy: Well, I'd like someone I have something in common with – who I can talk to easily.
Joe: I think I know just the girl for you: my cousin Lisa. She's a lot of fun and she loves sports, just like you.
Roy: Well, why not? I'll give it a try.
Joe: OK, I'll invite her over for dinner, and you can tell me what you think.

B Listen to Joe and Roy discuss Lisa after they had dinner together. What did Roy think of her?

3 GRAMMAR FOCUS

▶ **Relative pronouns**

As the subject of a clause
I like people **who/that** aren't too serious.
I like people **who/that** have a good sense of humor.

As the object of a clause
I want someone **(who/that)** I can have fun with.
I'd like someone **(who/that)** I can talk to easily.

GRAMMAR PLUS see page 132

A Match the information in columns A and B. Then compare with a partner.

A
1. I don't like to work with people who/that __c__
2. I have some good, old friends who/that __e__
3. I discuss my problems with people who/that __f__
4. I don't want to have a roommate who/that __b__
5. I'd like to have a boss who/that __d__
6. I enjoy teachers who/that __a__
7. I'm looking for a partner who/that __f__

B
a. help me understand things easily.
b. is messy.
c. are too competitive.
d. I can respect as a leader.
e. I met in middle school.
f. I have a lot in common with.
g. can give me good advice.

B Put a line through *who/that* in part A if it's optional. Then compare with a partner.

C **PAIR WORK** Complete the sentences in column A with your own information. Do you and your partner have similar opinions?

A: I don't like to work with people who are too competitive.
B: Neither do I. I like to work with people who are friendly and helpful.

4 WORD POWER Personality traits

A Match the words with the definitions. Then decide whether the words are positive (**P**) or negative (**N**). Write **P** or **N** after each word.

__h__ 1. easygoing __P__
__c__ 2. egotistical __N__
__e__ 3. inflexible __N__
____ 4. modest
__f__ 5. outgoing
__b__ 6. stingy __N__
__d__ 7. supportive __P__
____ 8. temperamental
__e__ 9. unreliable

a. a person who doesn't change easily and is stubborn
b. someone who doesn't like giving or spending money
c. someone who has a very high opinion of him- or herself
d. someone who is helpful and encouraging
e. a person who doesn't do what he or she promised
f. a person who enjoys being with other people
g. a person who has unpredictable or irregular moods
h. a person who doesn't worry much or get angry easily
i. someone who doesn't brag about his or her accomplishments

B **PAIR WORK** Cover the definitions. Take turns talking about the adjectives in your own words.

"An easygoing person is someone who . . ."

C **PAIR WORK** Think of at least two adjectives to describe your favorite relative. Then tell a partner.

That's my kind of friend! **3**

5 LISTENING What's new?

A Listen to conversations that describe three people. Are the descriptions positive (**P**) or negative (**N**)? Check (✓) the box.

		P	N
1.	Emma	☐	✓
2.	Mrs. Leblanc	✓	☐
3.	Pablo	✓	☐

B Listen again. Write two adjectives that describe each person in the chart.

6 DISCUSSION The right qualities

A What is the ideal friend, parent, or partner like? Add your own type of person under **People**. Then write one quality each ideal person should have, and one each should *not* have.

People	This person is . . .	This person is not . . .
The ideal friend		
The ideal parent		
The ideal partner		
The ideal _____		

B GROUP WORK Take turns describing your ideal people. Try to agree on the two most important qualities for each person.

A: I think the ideal friend is someone who is supportive and who is a good listener.
B: I agree. The ideal friend is someone who isn't critical . . .
C: Oh, I'm not sure I agree. . . .

7 WRITING A good friend

A Think about a good friend. Answer the questions. Then write a paragraph.

What is this person like?
How long have you known each other?
How did you meet?
How are you similar?
How are you different?
What makes your relationship special?

> My friend Nolan is easygoing and doesn't take life too seriously. He's someone who loves to have fun, and he makes sure everyone else has a good time, too. We met about six years ago . . .

B PAIR WORK Exchange paragraphs. How are your friends similar? How are they different?

Unit 1

8 PERSPECTIVES Are you difficult to please?

A Listen to some common complaints. Check (✓) the ones you agree with.

Do you get ANNOYED easily?
Take the quiz and find out.

- ☐ I can't stand it when a child screams in a restaurant.
- ☐ I can't stand it when I'm upset and people tell me to calm down.
- ☐ It bothers me when my doctor arrives late for an appointment.
- ☐ I don't like it when someone takes the last cookie without asking.
- ☐ It upsets me when a close friend forgets my birthday.
- ☐ I don't like it when people call me early in the morning on the weekend just to chat.
- ☐ It bothers me when a friend answers the phone at the dinner table.
- ☐ I hate it when people text the message "Call me."

Score: If you checked . . .

1–2 complaints: Wow! You don't get annoyed very easily.
3–4 complaints: You're fairly easygoing.
5–6 complaints: You get irritated pretty easily.
7–8 complaints: Relax! You get upset too easily.

B Calculate your score. Do you get annoyed easily?
Tell the class what bothers you the most.

9 PRONUNCIATION Linked sounds

A Listen and practice. Final consonant sounds are often linked to the vowel sounds that follow them.

It upsets me when a friend is late for an appointment.
I love it when a friend is supportive and kind.

B Mark the linked sounds in the sentences below. Listen and check. Then practice saying the sentences.

1. I hate it when a cell phone goes off at the movies.
2. I can't stand it when a person is inflexible.
3. Does it bother you when a friend is unreliable?

C **PAIR WORK** Take turns saying the sentences in Exercise 8. Pay attention to linked sounds.

That's my kind of friend! 5

10 GRAMMAR FOCUS

▶ *It* clauses + adverbial clauses with *when*

I like **it**	**when** my roommate cleans the apartment.
I don't mind **it**	**when** a friend answers the phone at the dinner table.
I can't stand **it**	**when** I'm upset and people tell me to calm down.
It makes me happy	**when** people do nice things for no reason.
It bothers me	**when** my doctor arrives late for an appointment.
It upsets me	**when** a close friend forgets my birthday.

GRAMMAR PLUS see page 132

A How do you feel about these situations? Complete the sentences with *it* clauses from the list. Then compare your sentences with a partner.

I love it	I don't mind it	It annoys me	It really upsets me
I like it	It doesn't bother me	I don't like it	I can't stand it
It makes me happy	I hate it		

1. _____ when a friend gives me a present for no special reason.
2. _____ when someone criticizes a friend of mine.
3. _____ when friends start arguing in front of me.
4. _____ when people call me late at night.
5. _____ when salesclerks are temperamental.
6. _____ when people are direct and say what's on their mind.
7. _____ when someone corrects my grammar in front of others.
8. _____ when a friend is sensitive and supportive.
9. _____ when people throw trash on the ground.
10. _____ when a friend treats me to dinner.

B **GROUP WORK** Do you ever get annoyed by a certain type of person or situation? Write down five things that annoy you the most. Then compare in groups.

A: I can't stand it when someone takes food off my plate.
B: I feel the same way. Especially when the person didn't order his or her own food!
C: Yeah, but it bothers me more when . . .

11 INTERCHANGE 1 Personality quiz

Interview a classmate to find out about his or her personality.
Go to Interchange 1 on page 114.

6 Unit 1

12 READING

A Are you a frequent social media user? What kinds of things get your attention on social media?

SOCIAL NETWORKS THAT AREN'T FOR EVERYONE

Since social networking websites first appeared, many have come and some have gone. However, their purpose has generally been the same: keeping up with old friends, making new friends, and sharing pictures, videos, and bits of interesting news. In addition, some sites make it possible to pursue new relationships, either online or in the real world.

For some people who have very specific interests, generic sites like Facebook or Twitter are not sufficient. They want to be part of a supportive online community that shares their particular passions.

A good example is Stache Passions, a social site for people who wear, admire, or have an interest in moustaches. It features photos of men with all sizes and styles of moustaches, forums for discussing the history, growing, and styling of the 'stache, and even a meet-up page to help you meet other moustache-lovers.

Purrsonals is a specialized site for those who love cats. Here you can meet and chat with cat-loving friends, set up feline play-dates with local people and their pets, and even find a home for a cat in need. And if your friends don't like it when you share endless cute cat videos on your regular social site, Purrsonals is where people are sure to appreciate them!

On a more serious note, Horyou is a website for people that want to do good in the world. On the site, you can connect with other social activists and entrepreneurs, plan meetings, share fund-raising strategies, and keep up with thousands of people who are working hard to make the world a better place. There are no funny videos here, but Horyou offers its own web-based video channel that features programs and documentaries about efforts to improve people's lives around the globe.

B Read the article. Which website is good for the people below? Write **S** (Stache Passions), **P** (Purrsonals), or **H** (Horyou).

This site would be good for someone who . . .
1. has a strong interest in personal appearance. _____
2. is hoping to adopt a new pet. _____
3. wants to watch a bit of light entertainment. _____
4. wants ideas for improving others' lives. _____
5. is interested in styles from the past. _____
6. wants to raise money for a charity. _____

C Find the words in the article that mean the following.
1. enough for a purpose _____
2. places where a discussion can take place _____
3. to like and be grateful for something _____
4. people who want to accomplish political or social change _____
5. plans of action _____

D PAIR WORK Do you belong to any specialized social networking sites? If yes, what is the focus? If not, what type of specialized site might you join?

That's my kind of friend! **7**

2 Working 9 to 5

▶ Discuss opinions, advantages, and disadvantages of jobs
▶ Compare various jobs

1 SNAPSHOT

What do you want from your career?

☐ Security
If you want to have stability, choose a job that you can keep for your whole life. You could be a federal judge, a public school teacher, or a university professor.

☐ Adventure
Perhaps you can't picture yourself doing the same thing, at the same place, for years and years. In that case, be something that will allow you to explore other places and other cultures, like an environmentalist or a tour guide.

☐ Money
Do you want to have a high-paying job? You may want to look into being a financial analyst, a doctor, or a stockbroker.

Rank the factors from 1 (most important) to 3 (least important). Compare with a partner.
Which factors did you consider when you chose your present job or your future career? Why?

2 PERSPECTIVES Career choices

A Listen to students discuss career choices. Do you agree or disagree? Check (✓) the speaker you agree with more.

- I'd like to work in the video game industry. Playing games all day would be lots of fun.
- I disagree! Playing the same game every day for months would be boring.
- Designing clothes is not a man's job. Women are much more fascinated by fashion.
- Being a flight attendant sounds very exciting. Traveling all the time would be really interesting.
- But flight attendants get tired of traveling. They spend most of their time in airports!
- That's not true! Many great fashion designers are men. Just look at Michael Kors!
- I'd enjoy working with animals. I think working as a veterinarian could be rewarding.
- I'm not so sure. Animals can be very unpredictable. Getting a dog bite would be scary!

B Compare your responses with your classmates. Give more reasons to support your opinions.

3 GRAMMAR FOCUS

Gerund phrases

Gerund phrases as subjects
Playing games all day would be lots of fun.
Being a flight attendant sounds exciting.
Designing clothes is not a man's job.
Working as a veterinarian could be rewarding.

Gerund phrases as objects
She'd be good at **testing games**.
He'd love **being a flight attendant**.
He wouldn't like **being a fashion designer**.
She'd enjoy **working with animals**.

GRAMMAR PLUS see page 133

A Look at the gerund phrases in column A. Write your opinion of each job by choosing information from columns B and C. Then add two more gerund phrases and write similar sentences.

A	B	C
1. working from home	seems	awful
2. doing volunteer work	could be	stressful
3. having your own business	would be	fantastic
4. working on a movie set	must be	fascinating
5. being a teacher	wouldn't be	pretty difficult
6. making a living as a tour guide	doesn't sound	kind of boring
7. taking care of sick people		really rewarding
8. retiring at age 40		very challenging
9. _____		
10. _____		

1. Working from home could be very challenging.

B **PAIR WORK** Give reasons for your opinions about the jobs in part A.

A: In my opinion, working from home could be very challenging.
B: Really? Why is that?
A: Because you have to learn to manage your time. It's easy to get distracted.
B: I'm not sure that's true. For me, working from home would be . . .

C **GROUP WORK** Complete the sentences with gerund phrases. Then take turns reading your sentences. Share the three most interesting sentences with the class.

1. I'd get tired of . . .
2. I'd be interested in . . .
3. I'd be very excited about . . .
4. I'd enjoy . . .
5. I think I'd be good at . . .
6. I wouldn't be very good at . . .

"I'd get tired of doing the same thing every day."

Working 9 to 5

4 WORD POWER Suffixes

A Add the suffixes -er, -or, -ist, or -ian to form the names of these jobs. Write the words in the chart and add one more example to each column.

| software develop _er_ | freelance journal___ | marketing direct___ | politic___ |
| computer technic___ | guidance counsel___ | project manag___ | psychiatr___ |

-er	-or	-ist	-ian
software developer			

B PAIR WORK Can you give a definition for each job?

"A software developer is someone who creates apps for computers and other devices."

5 SPEAKING Career paths

GROUP WORK Talk about a career you would like to have. Use information from Exercises 1–4 or your own ideas. Other students ask follow-up questions.

A: I'd enjoy working as a guidance counselor.
B: Why is that?
A: Helping kids must be really rewarding.
C: Where would you work?
A: Well, I think I'd like to work at a high school. I enjoy working with teens.

6 WRITING What's more satisfying?

A GROUP WORK What would you choose: a job that you love that doesn't pay well, or a high-paying job that you don't like? Discuss and list the consequences of the two alternatives.

B Use the list to write a paragraph justifying your choice.

> Having a high-paying job that you don't like could be very frustrating. First of all, you'd have to do something you don't like every day. You would have a lot of money. However, it's not worth it if . . .

useful expressions

First of all, . . .
In addition, . . .
Furthermore, . . .
For example, . . .
However, . . .
On the other hand, . . .
In conclusion, . . .

C PAIR WORK Read your partner's paragraph. Do you agree or disagree? Why or why not?

7 CONVERSATION It doesn't pay as much.

A Listen and practice.

Tyler: Guess what? . . . I've found a summer job!
Emma: That's great! Anything interesting?
Tyler: Yes, working at a beach resort.
Emma: Wow, that sounds fantastic!
Tyler: So, have *you* found anything?
Emma: Nothing yet, but I have a couple of leads. One is working as an intern for a news website – mostly answering emails and posts from readers. Or I can get a job as a camp counselor again.
Tyler: Being an intern sounds more challenging than working at a summer camp. You could earn college credits, and it's probably not as much work.
Emma: Yeah, but the internship doesn't pay as much as the summer camp job. Do they have another opening at the beach resort? That's the kind of job I'd really enjoy.

B Listen to the rest of the conversation. What is Tyler going to do at the resort?

8 GRAMMAR FOCUS

Comparisons

with adjectives
. . . sounds **more/less** challenging **than** . . .
. . . is hard**er than** . . .
. . . is **not as** hard **as** . . .

with nouns
. . . has **better/worse** hours **than** . . .
. . . has **more** education **than** . . .
. . . is**n't as much** work **as** . . .

with verbs
. . . earns **more/less than** . . .
. . . earns **as much as** . . .
. . . does**n't** pay **as much as** . . .

with past participles
. . . is **better** paid **than** . . .
. . . is **as well** paid **as** . . .
. . . is**n't as** well paid **as** . . .

GRAMMAR PLUS see page 133

A Complete the sentences using the words in parentheses. Compare with a partner. (More than one answer is possible.)

1. In my opinion, being a firefighter is _____ (stressful) being a sales associate. In addition, sales associates have _____ (hours) firefighters.
2. In general, doctors need _____ (training) nutritionists. However, they usually _____ (earn) nutritionists.
3. Game testers don't need _____ (experience) software developers. As a result, they _____ (earn) software developers.
4. A career in banking is often _____ (demanding) a career in sales, but it is also _____ (paid).

B **PAIR WORK** Compare the jobs in part A. Which would you choose? Why?

Working 9 to 5 11

9 PRONUNCIATION Stress with compound nouns

A Listen and practice. Notice that the first word in these compound nouns has more stress. Then add two more compound nouns to the chart.

•	•	•	•
firefighter	game tester	guidance counselor	
hairstylist	flight attendant	project manager	

B GROUP WORK Which job in each column would be more challenging? Why? Tell the group. Pay attention to stress.

10 LISTENING It's not what I thought.

A Listen to Caden talk to Janelle about his job as a video game tester. Which parts of the job does he like and dislike? Check (✓) Like or Dislike.

		Like	Dislike
1.	The pay	☐	☐
2.	The hours	☐	☐
3.	Testing games	☐	☐
4.	Playing video games at home	☐	☐
5.	Thinking of new ideas for games	☐	☐

B Listen again. What does Caden decide to do?

C PAIR WORK What other advice would you give Caden?

11 DISCUSSION Which job would you take?

A What is a job you would like to have? What is a job you wouldn't like to have? Write each one on a separate slip of paper.

> kindergarten teacher   tour guide

B GROUP WORK Mix all the slips from your group. One student picks two slips and the group helps him or her decide between the two jobs.

A: You should take the job as a kindergarten teacher because you enjoy working with kids.
B: But being a tour guide sounds more exciting. I could travel more and earn more money.
C: But you'd work longer hours and . . .

12 INTERCHANGE 2 Networking

Would you be a good party planner? Go to Interchange 2 on page 115.

12 Unit 2

13 READING

A Skim the web posts. Which person works in the most traditional workplace? the least traditional?

THE PERFECT WORKPLACE?
What is your workplace like? Tell us and see how other places compare!

My workplace is cooler than any office I've ever seen. Working here is really stimulating. I share a table with my co-workers, and the workplace is flooded with light. Getting free meals is great, and there are relaxing activities like billiards and board games. Plus we get a membership to a local gym! It isn't all play, of course – we work very hard – but the perks make it better than any other job I can imagine.
Lauren L., Palo Alto, California

When I got my job as a project manager for a finance company in London, I imagined a modern building with views of the city and open workspaces. When I arrived for my first day, I was pretty surprised. I found a typical cubicle farm, with desks as far as the eye could see. It works for me, though. I can concentrate in my own space and then talk with colleagues in the meeting rooms. We do have a great gym on the ground floor, so that's a bonus!
Catherine D., London, UK

I work in a research laboratory at a botanical garden. Working in a lab isn't as tedious as it sounds. That's because a lot of my work takes place in the greenhouses or outdoors. I love spending time among plants, and I enjoy working with other scientists who share my interests. True, the workplace isn't very luxurious. We have a tiny break room that some people complain about, and there isn't a place to work out or anything, but being outdoors so much makes up for the disadvantages.
Mark T., Bronx, New York

B Read the web posts. Who would have written these sentences about their workplace? Write the names.

1. Working in different environments keeps me from getting bored. _____
2. It's a perfect environment for sharing new ideas with co-workers. _____
3. There's nothing unique about it, but it's fine for the kind of work we do. _____
4. Visitors might get the idea that we don't take our work seriously. _____
5. Some employees are dissatisfied with the workplace, but I don't mind it. _____
6. I love being able to exercise without leaving the building. _____

C Find the words below in the web posts. Then complete the sentences with the words.

| stimulating | perk | cubicle | tedious | luxurious |

1. One _perk_ of my job is that we get free tickets to cultural and sporting events.
2. Working with creative people is very _sti_____ because we can share lots of great ideas!
3. The disadvantage of working in a _cubica___ is that you can hear everything that's going on around you.
4. The marketing director's office is very _luxurio__, with beautiful furniture and valuable paintings.
5. Working with numbers all day seems _tediony_ to some people, but I enjoy it.

D **PAIR WORK** Which of the workplaces would you like the best? What features of a workplace matter most to you?

Working 9 to 5

Units 1–2 Progress check

SELF-ASSESSMENT

How well can you do these things? Check (✓) the boxes.

I can . . .	Very well	OK	A little
Describe personalities (Ex. 1)	☐	☐	☐
Ask about and express preferences (Ex. 1)	☐	☐	☐
Understand and express complaints (Ex. 2)	☐	☐	☐
Give opinions about jobs (Ex. 3)	☐	☐	☐
Describe and compare different jobs (Ex. 4)	☐	☐	☐

1 SPEAKING Doing things together

A What two qualities would you like someone to have for these situations?

A person to . . .
1. be your business partner _____ _____
2. share an apartment with _____ _____
3. go on vacation with _____ _____
4. work on a class project with _____ _____

B CLASS ACTIVITY Find someone you could do each thing with.

A: What kind of person would you like to be your business partner?
B: I'd choose someone who has initiative and is hardworking.
A: Me, too! And I'd like someone who I can . . .

2 LISTENING I know what you mean!

A Listen to Suki and Andy discuss these topics. Complete the chart.

	Andy's biggest complaint	Suki's biggest complaint
1. websites		
2. children		
3. taxi drivers		
4. restaurant servers		

B PAIR WORK What is your biggest complaint about any of the topics in part A?

"I hate it when you can't find the products you want on a company's website."

14

3 SURVEY Job evaluation

A GROUP WORK What job would you like to have? Ask and answer questions in groups to complete the chart.

	Name	Job	Good points	Bad points
1.				
2.				
3.				
4.				

A: What job would you like to have?
B: I'd like to be a flight attendant.
C: What would be the good points?
B: Well, traveling around the world would be exciting.
D: Would there be any bad points?
B: Oh, sure. I'd dislike packing and unpacking all the time. . . .

useful expressions

I would(n't) be good at . . .
I would enjoy/dislike . . .
I would(n't) be interested in . . .
I would(n't) be excited about . . .

B GROUP WORK Who thought of the most unusual job? the best job? the worst job?

4 ROLE PLAY Choosing a job

Student A: Your partner, Student B, is looking for a job. Based on his or her opinions about jobs in Exercise 3, suggest two other jobs that Student B might enjoy.

Student B: You are looking for a job. Student A suggests two jobs for you. Discuss the questions below. Then choose one of the jobs.

Which one is more interesting? harder?
Which one has better hours? better pay?
Which job would you rather have?

A: I thought of two other jobs for you. You could be a hairstylist or a truck driver.
B: Hmm. Which job has better hours?
A: Well, a hairstylist has better hours, but it's not as . . .

Change roles and try the role play again.

WHAT'S NEXT?

Look at your Self-assessment again. Do you need to review anything?

3 Lend a hand.

▶ Discuss favors, borrowing, and lending
▶ Leave messages with requests

1 SNAPSHOT

ANNOYING FAVORS PEOPLE ASK

Could you . . .

1. babysit my kids on the weekend?
2. watch my stuff for a few minutes?
3. let me use your credit card?
4. drive me to the airport?
5. let me use your passcode to download a movie?
6. help me move to my new apartment?
7. come with me to my niece's school concert?
8. let me stay at your place for a couple of weeks?
9. donate to my favorite charity?
10. co-sign a bank loan for me?

Imagine that a close friend asked you each of these favors. Which would you agree to do? What are three other favors that you dislike being asked?

2 CONVERSATION Thanks a million.

A Listen and practice.

Carlos: Hey, Keiko. What's up?
Keiko: Hi, Carlos. I was wondering if you could help me. I'm moving to my new apartment this weekend, and my car is pretty small. Can I borrow your truck, please?
Carlos: Um, I need it on Saturday, but you can borrow it on Sunday.
Keiko: Thanks so much.
Carlos: Sure. So, have you packed already?
Keiko: Uh-huh. I mean, I'll have everything packed by Sunday. You know, I think some of my boxes are going to be kind of heavy. Would you mind helping me put them in your truck on Sunday?
Carlos: I guess not. I suppose you want my help taking them out of the truck, too?
Keiko: Oh, that'd be great. Thanks a million, Carlos!

B Listen to two more calls Keiko makes. What else does she need help with? Do her friends agree to help?

3 GRAMMAR FOCUS

Requests with modals, *if* clauses, and gerunds

Less formal
Can I borrow your truck, please?
Could you lend me your truck, please?
Is it OK if I use your credit card?
Do you mind if I use your credit card?
Would it be all right if I us**ed** your credit card?
Would you mind if I borrow**ed** your truck?
Would you mind help**ing** me on Sunday?
More formal
I was wondering if you **could** help me move.

GRAMMAR PLUS see page 134

A Circle the correct answers. Then practice with a partner.

1. **A: Is it OK if / Would / Do you mind** I use your cell phone? Mine just died.
   B: No problem, but can you keep it short? I'm expecting an important phone call.

2. **A:** Would you mind if I **stay / staying / stayed** at your place for the weekend?
   B: Not at all. It'll be fun to have you stay with us.

3. **A:** I was wondering **I could / if I could / if I would** borrow your car tomorrow.
   B: Sure, that's fine. Just be careful. I've only had it for a couple of months.

4. **A:** Could you **lend / lending / lent** me $20?
   B: I'm sorry. I don't have any money to spare right now.

5. **A:** Would you mind **help / helped / helping** me pack my stuff this weekend?
   B: No, I don't mind. I'm not doing anything then.

6. **A: Would you mind / Can / Is it OK if** you feed my cats while I'm on vacation, please?
   B: Sorry, I don't get along with cats.

B Rewrite these sentences to make them more formal requests. Then practice making your requests with a partner. Accept or decline each request.

1. Come to my cousin's wedding with me.
2. Can I borrow your notes to study for the test?
3. Can you lend me your camera to take with me on my vacation?
4. Drive me to the airport.
5. Help me paint my apartment.
6. I'd like to borrow your cell phone to call a friend in London.

1. *Would you mind coming to my cousin's wedding with me?*

Lend a hand. **17**

4 PRONUNCIATION Unreleased consonants

A Listen and practice. Notice that when /t/, /d/, /k/, /g/, /p/, and /b/ are followed by other consonant sounds, they are unreleased.

Could Craig take care of my pet skunk?
Can you ask Bob to help me?

B Circle the unreleased consonants in the conversations. Listen and check. Then practice the conversations with a partner.

1. **A:** I was wondering if I could borrow that book.
   B: Yes, but can you take it back to Doug tomorrow?
2. **A:** Would you mind giving Albert some help moving that big bed?
   B: Sorry, but my doctor said my back needs rest.

5 LISTENING I was wondering . . .

A Listen to three telephone conversations. Write down what each caller requests. Does the other person agree to the request? Check (✓) Yes or No.

	Request	Yes	No
1. Jesse			
2. Liz			
3. Min-jun			

B PAIR WORK Use the chart to act out each conversation in your own words.

6 WRITING A message with requests

A Write a message to a classmate asking for several favors. Explain why you need help.

B PAIR WORK Exchange messages. Write a reply accepting or declining the requests.

Home   Profile   Contacts   Address book   Chats   Sign out

Sara
Hi, Kim! Could I ask you a few small favors? I'm planning to spend this weekend at the beach. I was wondering if I could borrow your sleeping bag. Also, . . .

Kim
Sorry, Sara, but I can't help you this time. First of all, I lent my sleeping bag to my brother, and he hasn't returned it yet. . . .

18 Unit 3

7 INTERCHANGE 3 Beg and borrow

Find out how generous you are. Go to Interchange 3 on page 116.

8 WORD POWER Verb-noun collocations

A Which verb is not usually paired with each noun? Put a line through the verb. Then compare with a partner.

1. return / do / ask for / ~~make~~ — a favor
2. owe / offer / do / accept — an apology
3. receive / accept / turn down / offer — an invitation
4. do / receive / give / accept — a gift
5. do / return / make / receive — a phone call
6. accept / make / decline / offer — a request
7. receive / return / do / give — a compliment

B PAIR WORK Add two questions to the list using the collocations in part A. Then take turns asking and answering the questions.

1. What are nice ways to return a favor? How do you usually return favors?
2. Have you ever invented an excuse to turn down an invitation? What excuse did you give?
3. When was the last time you declined a request? What was the request?
4. _____
5. _____

9 PERSPECTIVES Can you tell her . . . ?

A Listen to the requests people make at the school where Mary Martin teaches. Complete each request with *ask* or *tell*.

1. If you see Mary, can you _tell_ her that she left her phone in my car?
2. If you see Mary, could you _ask_ her whether or not she is coming to the teachers' meeting?
3. If you see Ms. Martin, can you _ask_ her if she's graded our tests yet?
4. If you see Mary, please _tell_ her not to forget the students' reports.
5. If you see Mary, could you _ask_ her to find me in the cafeteria after her meeting?
6. If you see Ms. Martin, would you _ask_ her what time I can talk to her about my homework?

B Who do you think made each request? the school coordinator? another teacher? a student?

Lend a hand. **19**

10 GRAMMAR FOCUS

Indirect requests — *Infinitive*

Statements
Mary, you left your phone in my car. →

Indirect requests introduced by *that*
Could you tell Mary (**that**) **she left her phone in my car**?

Imperatives
Mary, don't forget the students' reports. →

Indirect requests using infinitives
Can you tell Mary **not to forget the students' reports**?

Yes/No questions
Ms. Martin, have you graded our tests? →
Mary, are you coming to the meeting? →

Indirect requests introduced by *if* or *whether*
Can you ask her **if she's graded our tests yet**?
Could you ask her **whether or not she is coming to the meeting**?

Wh-questions
Mary, where are you having lunch? →
Ms. Martin, what time can I talk to you about my homework? →

Indirect requests introduced by a question word
Can you ask Mary **where she's having lunch**?
Would you ask her **what time I can talk to her about my homework**?

GRAMMAR PLUS *see page 134*

Read the things people want to say to Mary. Rewrite the sentences as indirect requests. Then compare with a partner.

1. Mary, did you get my message about your phone?
2. Mary, will you give me a ride to school tomorrow?
3. Ms. Martin, when is our assignment due?
4. Mary, why didn't you meet us at the cafeteria for lunch?
5. Ms. Martin, I won't be in class tomorrow night.
6. Mary, are you going to the school party on Saturday?
7. Mary, please return my call when you get your phone back.
8. Mary, have you received my wedding invitation?

1. Could you ask Mary if she got my message about her phone?

11 SPEAKING No problem.

A Write five requests for your partner to pass on to classmates.

> Would you ask Keith if he can turn off his phone in class?

B CLASS ACTIVITY Ask your partner to pass on your requests. Go around the class and make your partner's requests. Then tell your partner how people responded.

A: Would you ask Keith if he can turn off his phone in class?
B: No problem. . . . Keith, could you turn off your cell phone in class?
C: I'm sorry, but I can't! I'm expecting an important phone call.
B: Lee, Keith says he's expecting an important phone call.

12 READING

A Scan the article. What are the three problems?

CAN YOU TELL IT LIKE IT IS?

There are some things that are almost impossible to say to our close friends – especially if we want <u>them</u> to be our friends for life. Are you wondering what problems others have with bringing up difficult subjects? Read on.

1. "I can't stand your other friends."

My best friend sometimes hangs out with some people that I really don't like. I think they have a bad influence on her, and she only spends time with them because they are "cool." Could you tell me if I should bring <u>the matter</u> up with her, or if it would be better for me to keep quiet? I don't want to lose her as a friend. – Carly

2. "I won't help you cheat."

My closest friend has lost interest in school and studying. He says he's bored with <u>the whole thing</u>, so he often asks me whether I'll do him a favor and let him copy my homework. So far I've said no, but he keeps asking me. I told him that I think we'll get in trouble, but he just laughed and told me not to worry. I don't want to put my grades at risk, but I'm afraid to confront my friend about <u>this</u>, so I just keep avoiding the topic. How can I get him to stop asking? I was wondering if you could give me some tips for handling my problem. – Matt

3. "No, I CAN'T do that for you!"

My best friend and I get along really well, but she is constantly asking me to do things for her. "Could you help me pick out some new clothes? Would you mind if I borrowed your car? Can you look after my apartment while I'm away?" And <u>these</u> are just a few examples. I've said yes so many times that now I'm afraid I'll hurt her feelings if I say no. Any ideas? – Dana

B Read the article. Then answer the questions.

1. Why is Carly concerned about her friend? _____
2. What is Matt most worried about? _____
3. Why is Dana afraid to say no to her friend? _____
4. Who is this advice best for?
    a. Say that you know your friend can handle the work himself. _____
    b. Agree to some requests, but only if your friend does something in return. _____
    c. Tell your friend there are more important things than being popular. _____

C What do the underlined words in the article refer to? Write the correct word(s).

1. them _____
2. the matter _____
3. the whole thing _____
4. this _____
5. these _____

D **PAIR WORK** Have you ever had similar problems with friends? How were the problems resolved? What advice would you give to Carly, Matt, and Dana?

Lend a hand. **21**

4 What happened?

▶ Describe past events
▶ Tell stories

1 SNAPSHOT

NEWS
Several Streets Closed After "Suspicious Package" Was Found

HEALTH
Why Weight Loss Isn't the Same as Being Healthy

TRENDING TOPICS
The Earth Is Getting Warmer and the Signs Are Everywhere

ARTS
The Top-Rated TV Shows You Need to Be Watching Right Now

SCIENCE
Women Need More Sleep Than Men Because They Use More of Their Brains

TECH
Here Are the Five Must-Have Apps for Runners

Which story would you like to read? Why?
What types of stories do you usually read online?
Where do you get your news? What's happening in the news today?

2 PERSPECTIVES Listen up.

A Listen to what people are listening to on their way to work. Which stories from Exercise 1 are they related to?

Hey, I just downloaded this incredible app. I used it this morning and I think you're going to love it. While I was working out, it calculated exactly how many calories I burned. The bad thing is, it tells me I still need to run about 4 miles to burn off last night's dinner.

As scientists were doing some research on the effects of sleep deprivation, they discovered that women need about 20 more minutes of sleep a night than men do. They think the reason is that women tend to do several tasks at once, which makes their brains work harder.

Hi, Jeff. We're canceling our meeting in the downtown office this morning. We just learned that the police have closed all the streets in the area. It seems that a man was looking for his lost cat when he found a suspicious package inside a trash can. In the end, it was just an old box of chocolates.

B Which is a message from a co-worker? a message from a friend? a podcast?

22

3 GRAMMAR FOCUS

▶ Past continuous vs. simple past

Use the past continuous for an ongoing action in the past.
Use the simple past for an event that interrupts that action.

Past continuous	Simple past
While I **was working** out,	it **calculated** how many calories I burned.
As scientists **were doing** research,	they **discovered** that women need more sleep than men.
A man **was looking** for his cat	when he **found** a suspicious package inside a trash can.

GRAMMAR PLUS see page 135

A Complete the stories using the past continuous or simple past forms of the verbs. Then compare with a partner.

1. **Bad memory, bad luck:** Marcia Murphy _____ (donate) her old pants to a thrift shop. As she _____ (walk) home, she _____ (remember) she _____ (leave) $20 in her pants pocket.

2. **Good intentions, bad interpretation:** Jason Clark _____ (walk) home one day, when he _____ (see) a little puppy crying on the sidewalk, so he _____ (stop) to help. As he _____ (pick) him up, a woman _____ (come) from nowhere screaming: "Stop that guy. He's trying to steal my puppy." Jason _____ (end) up spending three hours at the police station.

3. **A bad ride, a bad fall:** On her birthday last year, Diane Larson _____ (drive) to work when she _____ (have) a bad accident. This year, just to be safe, she decided to stay home on her birthday. Unfortunately, that night while she _____ (sleep) in her apartment, the floor of her living room _____ (collapse) and she _____ (fall) into her neighbor's apartment.

B GROUP WORK Take turns retelling the stories in part A. Add your own ideas and details to make the stories more interesting!

4 PRONUNCIATION Intonation in complex sentences

▶ A Listen and practice. Notice how each clause in a complex sentence has its own intonation pattern.

As Marcia was walking home, she remembered she left $20 in her pants pocket.

A man was looking for his cat when he found a package.

B PAIR WORK Use your imagination to make complex sentences. Take turns starting and finishing the sentences. Pay attention to intonation.

A: As Lee was coming to school today . . .
B: . . . he saw a parade coming down the street.

What happened? 23

5 LISTENING Crazy but true!

A Listen to three news stories. Number the pictures from 1 to 3. (There is one extra picture.)

B Listen again. Take notes on each story.

	Where did it happen?	When did it happen?	What happened?
1.			
2.			
3.			

6 WRITING A personal account

A Think of a story that happened to you or to someone you know. Choose one of the titles below, or create your own.

A Scary ExperienceI'll Never Forget That Day
I Was Really LuckyI Can't Believe It Happened

B Write your story. First, answer these questions.

Who was involved?Where did it happen?
When did it happen?What happened?

I Was Really Lucky

Last year, I took a trip to see my grandparents. I was waiting in the airport for my flight when a storm hit, and all the flights were cancelled. Luckily, I . . .

C GROUP WORK Take turns telling your stories. Other students ask questions. Who has the best story?

24 Unit 4

7 CONVERSATION That's terrible!

A Listen and practice.

CAROL Guess what? Someone stole my new bike yesterday!

MILO Oh, no! What happened?

CAROL Well, I was having lunch with a friend, and I had parked it on the street, just like I always do. When I came back, someone had stolen it. I guess I'd forgotten to lock it up.

MILO That's terrible! Did you report the theft to the police?

CAROL Yes, I did. And I also listed it on that site for stolen and lost bikes. But I doubt I'll ever get it back.

B Listen to the rest of the conversation. What did Milo have stolen once? Where was he?

8 GRAMMAR FOCUS

Past perfect

Use the past perfect for an event that occurred before another event in the past.

Past event	Past perfect event
I **was having** lunch with a friend,	and I **had parked** my bike on the street.
When I **came back,**	someone **had stolen** it.
They **were able** to steal it	because I **had forgotten** to lock it up.

GRAMMAR PLUS see page 135

A Write the correct verbs to complete the sentences. Then compare with a partner.

1. I ____took____ (took/had taken) a trip to London last year. I was a bit scared because I _____ (didn't travel/hadn't traveled) abroad before, but everything was perfect.
2. I _____ (visited/was visiting) the British Museum one afternoon when I _____ (ran/had run) into an old school friend who I _____ (didn't see/hadn't seen) for over 10 years.
3. One weekend, we _____ (were driving/had driven) to Liverpool when we _____ (ran/were running) out of gas on the highway because we _____ (forgot/had forgotten) to fill up the tank before leaving. Fortunately, a truck driver _____ (stopped/had stopped) and _____ (helped/had helped) us.
4. On the last day, as I _____ (was going/had gone) up to my hotel room, I _____ (got/had gotten) stuck in the elevator. After I _____ (was/had been) stuck for an hour, someone _____ (started/had started) it again.

B **PAIR WORK** Complete the sentences with your own ideas.

Until last year, I had never . . .
One day, as I was . . .

What happened? **25**

9 WORD POWER Exceptional events

A Match the words in column A with the definitions in column B.

A
1. coincidence _____
2. dilemma _____
3. disaster _____
4. emergency _____
5. lucky break _____
6. mishap _____
7. mystery _____
8. triumph _____

B
a. an unexpected event that brings good fortune
b. a situation that involves a difficult choice
c. something puzzling or unexplained
d. an event that causes suffering or destruction
e. a great success or achievement
f. an accident, mistake, or unlucky event
g. a sudden, dangerous situation that requires quick action
h. a situation when two similar things happen at the same time for no reason

B PAIR WORK Choose one kind of event from part A. Write a situation for it.

> A man bought an old house for $10,000. As he was cleaning the attic of his new home, he found an old painting by a famous painter. He had never collected art, but when he took it to a museum, he found out it was worth almost one million dollars. (lucky break)

C GROUP WORK Read your situation. Can others guess which kind of event it describes?

10 SPEAKING It's a story about . . .

GROUP WORK Have you ever experienced the events in Exercise 9, part A? Tell your group about it. Answer any questions.

A: It's a story about a coincidence.
B: What happened?
A: My sister bought a new dress for her graduation party. She had saved for months to buy it. When she got to the party, another girl was wearing the exact same dress!
C: Wow! That's more than a coincidence. It's a disaster! And what did she do?

11 INTERCHANGE 4 Spin a yarn

Tell a story. Go to Interchange 4 on page 117.

26 Unit 4

12 READING

A Skim the article. Was the story about lice true or false?

Believing More Than We Should

Is everything you read on the Internet true? If your answer is "no," you are absolutely right. Many stories and even photos are not to be trusted. And don't believe that because a good friend or a well-known news source has posted something that it is necessarily trustworthy.

There are many reasons for the spread of inaccurate content on the Internet. One reason is that satirical websites can create very believable stories, which they invent in order to make a point or to make people laugh. Other reasons might be an attempt to gain more readers, a desire to damage someone's reputation, or simple curiosity about how far a fake story can spread.

One story that spread throughout the media before anyone had checked the facts involved teenagers, selfies, and head lice. The article claimed that when teenagers were posing together for selfies, their heads often touched and the tiny insects were jumping from head to head. The article went on to say that this was causing a massive outbreak of lice. Some major websites and news outlets picked up the story, not even bothering to consult the experts. It turned out that some entrepreneurs who were marketing a new treatment for head lice had made up the story and posted it. Their motivation was to get attention and more business.

The spread of this story is understandable. It involved one epidemic (selfies) causing another (lice), and the "ick" factor was irresistible. Because there is so much false information online, there are now websites, such as *Snopes* and *Factcheck*, which exist specifically to find out if stories are true or not. So the next time you see a story that sounds too good to be true, at least you have somewhere to turn for verification before you spread false information to all your friends.

B Read the article. Find the words in italics in the article. Then check (✓) the meaning of each word.

1. *inaccurate*   ☐ not exact or true   ☐ shocking or disgusting
2. *satirical*   ☐ humorously critical   ☐ completely factual
3. *reputation*   ☐ hurtful news about someone ☐ public opinion of someone
4. *massive*   ☐ small   ☐ very large
5. *irresistible* ☐ hard to prove   ☐ hard to fight against
6. *verification* ☐ proof of truth   ☐ another opinion

C **PAIR WORK** Discuss these questions.

Do you think you would have believed the story about selfies and head lice?
Do you think the creation of the story was justified or not?
Who do you think is most responsible for the story being so popular?
Do you think there should be a penalty for spreading false information? If so, what should it be?

D **GROUP WORK** Have you ever read a story that turned out to be false? How did you find out the truth?

Units 3–4 Progress check

SELF-ASSESSMENT

How well can you do these things? Check (✓) the boxes.

I can . . .	Very well	OK	A little
Discuss favors (Ex. 1)	☐	☐	☐
Leave messages with requests (Ex. 2)	☐	☐	☐
Tell a story, making clear the sequence of events (Ex. 3, 5)	☐	☐	☐
Understand the sequence of events in a story (Ex. 4)	☐	☐	☐

1 ROLE PLAY Save the date!

Student A: You are planning a class party at your house. Think of three things you need help with. Then call a classmate and ask for help.

Student B: Student A is planning a party. Agree to help with some things, but not everything.

"Hi, Martina. I'm calling about the party. Would you mind . . . ?"

Change roles and try the role play again.

2 DISCUSSION Who said it?

A GROUP WORK Take turns reading each request. Then discuss the questions and come up with possible answers.

> Tell Rita that I'm going to be a half hour late for our meeting. Ask her to wait for me in her office.

> Tell your officers that he's white and wears a blue collar with his name on it – Rex. Please call if you find him.

> I'm sorry to bother you, but I really need it back for the office party on Friday. Please ask Sue to bring it over before that.

1. What is the situation?
2. Who is the request for? Who do you think received the request and passed it on?
3. Give an indirect request for each situation.

"Could you tell Rita . . . ?"

B CLASS ACTIVITY Compare your answers. Which group has the most interesting answers for each message?

3 SPEAKING And then . . . ?

A PAIR WORK Choose a type of event from the box. Then make up a title for a story about it. Write the title on a piece of paper.

| disaster   emergency   lucky break   mystery   triumph |

B PAIR WORK Exchange titles with another pair. Discuss the questions *who, what, where, when, why,* and *how* about the other pair's title. Then make up a story.

C Share your story with the pair who wrote the title.

<u>The Mystery of the Message in a Bottle</u>

I was walking on the beach when I saw a bottle with a message inside. The bottle looked very old, and it was hard to open it. Inside there was a message: "My beloved Catherine, I hope you . . ."

4 LISTENING What happened first?

▶ Listen to each situation. Number the events from 1 to 3.

1. ☐ She got sick.　　☐ She went on vacation.　　☐ She went back to work.
2. ☐ John called me.　　☐ I didn't get the message.　　☐ I changed phone numbers.
3. ☐ I was very nervous.　　☐ I left the office.　　☐ I felt relieved.
4. ☐ We went out.　　☐ My cousin stopped by.　　☐ I was watching a movie.

5 DISCUSSION Beginning, middle, and end

GROUP WORK Choose the beginning of a story from column A and an ending from column B. Discuss interesting or unusual events that could link A to B. Then make up a story.

A
Once, I . . .
accepted an interesting invitation.
was asked to do an unusual favor.
received an unexpected phone call.
owed someone a big apology.

B
Believe it or not, . . .
I got home, and there were 30 people in my living room!
I had no idea where I was.
when I got there, everyone had left.
it was the star of my favorite TV show!

A: Once, I accepted an interesting invitation.
B: Let's see. . . . I was biking home when I got a text from an old friend.
C: I hadn't seen him in over five years.
D: I was really surprised, but . . .

WHAT'S NEXT?

Look at your Self-assessment again. Do you need to review anything?

5 Expanding your horizons

▶ Discuss living in a foreign country
▶ Describe cultural expectations and differences

1 PERSPECTIVES Challenges of living abroad

A Listen to people talk about moving to a foreign country. Check (✓) the concerns you think you would share.

☐ "One thing that I'd really miss is hanging out with my friends." _____
☐ "Something that I'd be worried about is the local food. I'm a picky eater." _____
☐ "Getting used to a different culture might be difficult at first." _____
☐ "I'd be worried about not knowing how to get around in a new city." _____
☐ "The people that I'd miss the most are my parents. We're very close." _____
☐ "Not knowing the local customs is something I'd be concerned about." _____
☐ "I'd be nervous about getting sick and not knowing how to explain my symptoms." _____
☐ "Communicating in a foreign language could be a challenge." _____

B Rate each concern from 1 (not worried at all) to 5 (really worried). What would be your biggest concern? Why?

2 WORD POWER Mixed feelings

A These words are used to describe how people sometimes feel when they live in a foreign country. Which are positive (**P**)? Which are negative (**N**)? Write P or N.

anxious	N	embarrassed	N	insecure	N
comfortable	P	enthusiastic	P	nervous	N
confident	P	excited	P	uncertain	N
curious	P	fascinated	P	uncomfortable	N
depressed	N	homesick	N	worried	N

B **GROUP WORK** Tell your group about other situations in which you experienced the feelings in part A. What made you feel that way? How do you feel about the situations now?

A: I felt very embarrassed yesterday. I fell down the stairs in a restaurant.
B: How did it happen?
A: I think I slipped on something.
C: Did you get hurt?
A: Just a couple of bruises, but the restaurant manager was worried, so he convinced me to go to the hospital.

confident

3 GRAMMAR FOCUS

▶ Noun phrases containing relative clauses

Something (that) I'd be worried about is the local food.
One thing (that) I'd really miss is hanging out with my friends.
The people (who/that) I'd miss the most are my parents.

The local food is **something (that) I'd be worried about**.
Hanging out with my friends is **one thing (that) I'd really miss**.
My parents are **the people (who/that) I'd miss the most**.

GRAMMAR PLUS see page 136

A Complete the sentences about living in a foreign country. Use the phrases below. Then compare with a partner.

my friends	trying new foods	being away from home	getting lost in a new city
my family	feeling like an outsider	my grandmother's cooking	not understanding people
getting sick	making new friends	speaking a foreign language	learning about a different culture

1. . . . is something I'd be very enthusiastic about.
2. The thing I'd probably be most excited about is . . .
3. . . . is something I'd really miss.
4. Two things I'd be homesick for are . . .
5. Something I'd get depressed about is . . .
6. . . . is one thing that I might be embarrassed about.
7. The thing I'd feel most uncomfortable about would be . . .
8. . . . are the people who I'd miss the most.
9. One thing I'd be insecure about is . . .
10. . . . are two things I'd be anxious about.

B Now complete three sentences in part A with your own information.

1. Going to different festivals is something I'd be very enthusiastic about.

C GROUP WORK Rewrite your sentences from part B in another way. Then compare. Do others feel the same way?

1. I'd be very enthusiastic about going to different festivals.

4 PRONUNCIATION Word stress in sentences

▶ A Listen and practice. Notice that the important words in a sentence have more stress.

Uruguay is a country that I'd like to live in.

Speaking a foreign language is something I'd be anxious about.

Trying new foods is something I'd be curious about.

B PAIR WORK Mark the stress in the sentences you wrote in Exercise 3, part A. Then practice the sentences. Pay attention to word stress.

Expanding your horizons | 31

5 DISCUSSION Moving to a foreign country

GROUP WORK Read the questions. Think of two more questions to add to the list. Then take turns asking and answering the questions in groups.

What country would you like to live in? Why?
What country wouldn't you like to live in? Why?
Who is the person you would most like to go abroad with?
What is something you would never travel without?
Who is the person you would email first after arriving somewhere new?
What would be your two greatest concerns about living abroad?
What is the thing you would enjoy the most about living abroad?

A: What country would you like to live in?
B: The country I'd most like to live in is Zimbabwe.
C: Why is that?
B: Well, I've always wanted to work with wild animals. Besides, . . .

6 SNAPSHOT

ETIQUETTE TIPS FOR INTERNATIONAL TRAVELERS

CANADA: Always bring a small gift for the host when invited to a meal at a Canadian home.

RUSSIA: Do not turn down offers of food or drink.

JAPAN: Take off your shoes before entering a house.

FRANCE: When eating, don't rest your elbows on the table.

CHINA: Never point your chopsticks at another person.

BRAZIL: You can arrive between 15 to 30 minutes late for a party at a Brazilian friend´s home.

MOROCCO: Don't eat anything with your left hand.

THAILAND: Never touch a person's head.

Does your culture follow any of these customs?
Do any of these customs seem unusual to you? Explain.
What other interesting customs do you know?

32 Unit 5

7 CONVERSATION Bring a small gift.

A Listen and practice.

Klaus: My boss invited my wife and me to dinner at his house.
Olivia: Oh, how nice!
Klaus: Yes, but what do you do here when you're invited to someone's house?
Olivia: Well, here in the U.S., it's the custom to bring a small gift.
Klaus: Like what?
Olivia: Oh, maybe some flowers or chocolates.
Klaus: And is it all right to bring our kids along?
Olivia: Well, if you want to bring them, you're expected to ask if it's OK first.

B Listen to the rest of the conversation. If you are invited to someone's house in Germany, when are you expected to arrive? What can you bring as a gift?

8 GRAMMAR FOCUS

Expectations

When you visit someone,   it's the custom to bring a small gift.
                          you aren't supposed to arrive early.

If you want to bring others,   you're expected to ask if it's OK first.
                               you're supposed to check with the host.
                               it's not acceptable to bring them without asking.

GRAMMAR PLUS see page 136

A Match information in columns A and B to make sentences about customs in the United States and Canada. Then compare with a partner.

A
1. If someone sends you a gift, __e__
2. If you plan to visit someone at home, __a__
3. When you go out with friends for dinner, __f__
4. If the service in a restaurant is acceptable, __b__
5. When you meet someone for the first time, __c__
6. When you receive an invitation, __d__

B
a. you're supposed to call first.
b. it's the custom to leave a tip.
c. you aren't supposed to kiss him or her.
d. you're expected to respond to it quickly.
e. you're expected to thank the person.
f. it's acceptable to share the expenses.

B GROUP WORK How are the customs in part A different in your country?

C Complete these sentences with information about your country or a country you know well. Then compare with a partner.

1. In . . . , if people invite you to their home, . . .
2. When you go out on a date, . . .
3. If a friend is in the hospital, . . .
4. When you receive a gift, . . .
5. If you're staying at someone's home, . . .
6. When someone has a baby, . . .

Expanding your horizons 33

9 LISTENING Different cultures

A Listen to people describe customs they observed abroad. Complete the chart.

	Where was the person?	What was the custom?	How did the person react?
1. Carla			
2. Nate			
3. Shauna			

B PAIR WORK Which custom would you have the most trouble adapting to? Why?

10 SPEAKING Local customs

A PAIR WORK What should a visitor to your country know about local customs? Make a list. Include these points.

greeting and addressing someone
eating or drinking in public
taking photographs
giving gifts

dressing appropriately
visiting someone's home
using public transportation
tipping

When you ride in a cab, you're supposed to tip the driver.

B GROUP WORK Compare your lists with another pair. Then share experiences in which you (or someone you know) *didn't* follow the appropriate cultural behavior. What happened?

A: Once, when traveling abroad, I took a cab, and I didn't give the driver a tip.
B: What happened?
A: Well, he looked kind of angry. Then my friend gave the guy a tip, and I realized my mistake. It was a little embarrassing. . . .

11 WRITING A tourist pamphlet

A GROUP WORK Choose five points from the list you made in Exercise 10. Use them to write and design a pamphlet for tourists visiting your country or city.

WE HOPE YOU ENJOY YOUR STAY.

When you visit Italy, there are some important things you should know. For example, you can't buy a bus ticket on the bus in most big cities. Actually, you are supposed to . . .

B CLASS ACTIVITY Present your pamphlets. Which of the points were the most useful? What other information would a tourist need to know?

12 INTERCHANGE 5 Cultural dos and taboos

Compare customs in different countries. Go to Interchange 5 on page 118.

13 READING

A Scan the blog. What kinds of culture shock did the writer experience?

CULTURE SHOCK

I'm an exchange student from Spain navigating life in the United States. *Lucia M.*

PROFILE | PHOTOS | BLOG | COMMUNITY

JANUARY 15

My hometown of Seville, Spain is a city with active, passionate people and a lively nightlife, so coming to Seattle, in the United States, has been quite an eye-opener. Americans think of Seattle as an exciting city, but the first time I went out with friends on a Saturday night, there was hardly anybody out in the streets. I actually thought something was wrong! Then my friend explained that most of their social life takes place indoors. In Seville, people fill the streets year-round, and Saturday nights are like a big celebration.

JANUARY 22

After a couple of weeks of classes, I've begun to notice some differences between Spanish students and American students. In Spain, students talk a lot during class, and it's not always related to the lesson. On the other hand, when Spanish students are enthusiastic about a lesson, they often ask unusual questions, and it's common to stay after class to talk to the teacher. American students are expected to talk less and listen more, and many of them take detailed notes. Most of them leave the room as soon as the class ends, though, and are already focused on the next lesson.

FEBRUARY 8

Before I came to the United States, a friend who had studied here told me that American friends don't greet each other like we do in Spain, where we touch cheeks and make kissing sounds. Americans often hug each other, but kissing is not common, and I've gotten used to that. So imagine my surprise when I was introduced to a new girl, and she immediately gave me the Spanish-style double kiss. When I asked my friend about this later, she explained that the girl was from a family of actors, and that "air-kissing" was a usual greeting for artistic people. My friend also said that some outgoing people greet their friends or family this way, but that it would make other people feel uncomfortable. I think I'll stick to handshakes and hugs while I'm here!

B Read the blog. Then add the correct title to each entry.

Meeting and greeting   Where's the party?   Class contrasts

C Check (✓) True or False for each statement. Then correct the false statements.

	True	False	
1. The writer was nervous because the Seattle streets were crowded at night.	☐	☐	
2. Spanish students often stay after class to ask questions.	☐	☐	
3. Hugging is a usual greeting among friends in Spain.	☐	☐	
4. The writer plans to change the way she greets American friends.	☐	☐	

D **PAIR WORK** How do things in your city compare with Seville? with Seattle?

Expanding your horizons

6 That needs fixing.

▶ Describe problems and make complaints
▶ Discuss what needs fixing

1 SNAPSHOT

Some common complaints

Banking
The credit card company bills you for something you didn't buy.

Online shopping
The store sends you an incorrect size.

Internet providers
The Internet connection is not reliable, and you hardly ever get the speed you pay for.

Restaurants
The server rushes you to leave as soon as you finish your meal.

Vehicles
Your new car consumes too much gas.

Repair services
Your TV breaks again, a week after it was repaired.

Parking garage
Someone damages your car.

Have you ever had any of these problems? Which ones?
What would you do in each of these situations?
What other complaints have you had?

2 PERSPECTIVES That's not right!

A Listen to people describe complaints. Check (✓) what you think each person should do.

1. "I got a new suitcase, but when I arrived home, I noticed the lining was torn."
   ☐ take it back to the store
   ☐ ask the store to send you a new one

2. "My father sent me a coffee mug with my favorite team's logo, but when it arrived, it was chipped."
   ☐ tell your father about it
   ☐ contact the seller yourself

3. "I lent my ski pants to a friend, but when he returned them, there was a big stain on them."
   ☐ clean them yourself
   ☐ ask him to have them cleaned

4. "My boss borrowed my camera for a company event, and now the lens is scratched."
   ☐ talk to him or her about it
   ☐ say nothing and repair it yourself

5. "I bought a new washing machine just a month ago, and it's leaking already."
   ☐ ask for a refund
   ☐ send it back and get a new one

B Have you ever had similar complaints? What happened? What did you do?

3 GRAMMAR FOCUS

Describing problems 1

With past participles as adjectives

The suitcase lining is **torn**.
The car is **damaged**.
The coffee mug is **chipped**.
My pants are **stained**.
The camera lens is **scratched**.
The washing machine **is leaking**.*

With nouns

It has **a tear** in it./There's **a hole** in it.
There is **some damage** on the bumper.
There is **a chip** in it.
They have **a stain** on them.
There are **a few scratches** on it.
It has **a leak**.

*Exception: is leaking *is a present continuous form.*

GRAMMAR PLUS *see page 137*

A Read the comments from customers in a restaurant. Write sentences in two different ways using forms of the word in parentheses. Then compare with a partner.

1. Could we have another water pitcher? This one . . . (crack)
2. That valet was so careless. My car . . . (dent)
3. The toilet is dirty. And the sink . . . (leak)
4. This tablecloth isn't very clean. It . . . (stain)
5. Would you bring me another glass? This glass . . . (chip)
6. The table looks pretty dirty. The wood . . . , too. (scratch)
7. The server needs a new shirt. The one he's wearing . . . (tear)
8. The walls really need paint. And the ceiling . . . (damage)

1. *This one is cracked.*
   It has a crack.

B PAIR WORK Describe two problems with each thing below. Use forms of the words in the box. You may use the same word more than once.

| break | crack | damage | dent | leak | scratch | stain | tear |

A: The vase is broken.
B: Yes. And it has a crack, too.

C GROUP WORK Look around your classroom. How many problems can you describe?

"The floor is scratched, and the window is cracked. The desks are . . ."

That needs fixing. **37**

4 LISTENING I'd like a refund.

A Listen to three customers return items they purchased. Complete the chart.

	Did the store give a refund?	Why or why not?
1. Evie		
2. Darren		
3. Gisela		

B **GROUP WORK** How is your culture similar or different in terms of refunds and customer service?

5 ROLE PLAY How can I help you?

Student A: You are returning an item to a store. Decide what the item is and explain why you are returning it.

Student B: You are a salesperson. A customer is returning an item to the store. Ask these questions:

What exactly is the problem?   When did you buy it?
Can you show it to me?   Do you have the receipt?
Was it like this when you bought it?   Would you like a refund or a store credit?

Change roles and try the role play again.

6 CONVERSATION It needs to be adjusted.

A Listen and practice.

MR. LEROY Hello?

HEATHER Hello, Mr. Leroy. This is Heather Forman.

MR. LEROY Uh, Ms. Forman . . .

HEATHER In Apartment 12C.

MR. LEROY Oh, yes. What can I do for you? Does your refrigerator need fixing again?

HEATHER No, it's the oven this time.

MR. LEROY Oh. So, what's wrong with it?

HEATHER Well, I think the temperature control needs to be adjusted. The oven keeps burning everything I try to cook.

MR. LEROY Really? OK, I'll have someone look at it right away.

HEATHER Thanks a lot, Mr. Leroy.

MR. LEROY Uh, by the way, Ms. Forman, are you sure it's the oven and not your cooking?

B Listen to another tenant's call with Mr. Leroy. What's the tenant's problem?

38 Unit 6

7 GRAMMAR FOCUS

Describing problems 2

Need + gerund	Need + passive infinitive	Keep + gerund
The oven **needs adjusting**.	It **needs to be adjusted**.	Everything **keeps burning**.
The alarm **needs fixing**.	It **needs to be fixed**.	The alarm **keeps going off**.

GRAMMAR PLUS see page 137

A What needs to be done in this apartment? Write sentences about these items using *need* with gerunds or passive infinitives.

1. the cupboards (clean)
2. the fire alarm (adjust)
3. the lights (replace)
4. the plants (water)
5. the oven (fix)
6. the ceiling (paint)
7. the window (wash)
8. the light switch (change)

1. *The cupboards need cleaning.*
   OR
1. *The cupboards need to be cleaned.*

B PAIR WORK Think of five improvements you would like to make in your home. Which improvements will you most likely make? Which won't you make?

"First, the bedroom walls need painting. There are some small cracks. . . ."

8 WORD POWER Problems with electronics

A Circle the correct gerund to complete the sentences. Then compare with a partner.

1. My TV screen goes on and off all the time. It keeps **flickering** / **sticking**.
2. The music player app jumps to the next song every 20 seconds. It keeps **crashing** / **skipping**.
3. The battery in my new camera doesn't last long. It keeps **freezing** / **dying**.
4. Something is wrong with my computer! It keeps **crashing** / **jamming**.
5. I can't talk for long on my new phone. It keeps **dying** / **dropping** calls.
6. This printer isn't making all the copies I want. It keeps **jamming** / **flickering**.
7. My computer needs to be replaced. It keeps **dropping** / **freezing**.
8. The buttons on the remote control don't work well. They keep **skipping** / **sticking**.

B GROUP WORK Describe a problem with an electronic item you own. Don't identify it! Others will try to guess the item.

"Some keys on my device keep sticking, and some are loose. . . ."

That needs fixing. **39**

9 PRONUNCIATION Contrastive stress

A Listen and practice. Notice how a change in stress changes the meaning of each question and elicits a different response.

Is the **bedroom** window cracked?   (No, the kitchen window is cracked.)

Is the bedroom **window** cracked?   (No, the bedroom door is cracked.)

Is the bedroom window **cracked**?   (No, it's stuck.)

B Listen to the questions. Check (✓) the correct response.

1. a. Are my jeans torn?
   - ☐ No, they're stained.
   - ☐ No, your shirt is torn.
   b. Are my jeans torn?
   - ☐ No, they're stained.
   - ☐ No, your shirt is torn.

2. a. Is the computer screen flickering?
   - ☐ No, it's freezing.
   - ☐ No, the TV screen is flickering.
   b. Is the computer screen flickering?
   - ☐ No, it's freezing.
   - ☐ No, the TV screen is flickering.

10 LISTENING A throwaway culture

A Listen to a conversation between two friends. Answer the questions.

1. What is wrong with Hayley's phone? _____
2. What is Hayley's solution? _____
3. What is Aaron's solution? _____
4. Why doesn't Hayley like Aaron's solution? _____

B Listen again. What is a "throwaway culture"?

C GROUP WORK Do you agree that electronics aren't made as well as they used to be? Give an example to support your opinion.

11 WRITING A critical online review

A Imagine that you ordered a product online, but when you received it, you were unhappy with it. Write a critical online review. Explain all of the problems with the product and why you think others shouldn't buy it.

> **Best 4U promises a lot, delivers nothing.**
>
> I ordered a phone from Best 4U's website for my son's birthday. First, it took six weeks for the company to send it, and it arrived two weeks after his birthday. Now, the battery keeps dying very fast when he's just watching a movie or . . . READ MORE

B GROUP WORK Read your classmates' reviews. What would you do if you read this critical online review and worked for the company that sold the product?

12 INTERCHANGE 6 Home makeover

Do you have an eye for detail? Student A, go to Interchange 6A on page 119; Student B, go to Interchange 6B on page 120.

40 Unit 6

13 READING

A Skim the advice column. What problem did the reader have? How does the writer suggest solving the problem?

Home | Local | World | Entertainment | **Advice column**

Ask the Fixer!

Our problem-solver Marci Davis addresses a common problem with ride-sharing services.

After a meeting downtown, I used my phone to book a ride with a private car service in order to get home. As soon as the pick-up was confirmed, a friend came out of the building, spotted me, and offered me a ride home. I immediately canceled the car. But the next day I got an alert on my phone – the car service had charged my credit card $10! I contacted the service, and they said it was for a late cancellation. I didn't realize they were going to charge me for that! Can you fix this? – Lawrence, New York City

The fact is, Lawrence, that you need to read the terms of your ride-sharing app. It states clearly – somewhere in all those thousands of words – that when you cancel your ride less than ten minutes before your car is scheduled to arrive, you have to pay a fee. After all, the driver has already refused other possible passengers and is driving in your direction, so it's a loss when you cancel.

On the other hand, I do think something needs to be fixed. Do you know anyone who reads all the way through the terms of use for any app? There isn't enough time in the day! I talked to a representative at your ride-sharing company and made two suggestions. First, they need to highlight their cancellation policy at the beginning of the terms, where people will see it. Then, when you cancel a ride, a notification needs to be sent that tells you about the cancellation charge. That way, riders won't keep getting this annoying surprise. Let's hope the company pays attention.

What do you think? Post your comments, suggestions, complaints, and anecdotes.

B Read the advice column. Find the words in italics in the article. Then check (✓) the meaning of each word.

1. *confirm* ☐ make something available ☐ state that something will happen
2. *cancellation* ☐ act of stopping something ☐ act of delaying something
3. *representative* ☐ person who speaks for a company ☐ person who owns a company
4. *terms* ☐ rules of an agreement ☐ features of an app
5. *notification* ☐ act of giving information ☐ act of asking a question

C For each statement, check (✓) True, False, or Not given.

	True	False	Not given
1. Lawrence booked a ride by mistake.	☐	☐	☐
2. Lawrence did not expect to be charged for his ride.	☐	☐	☐
3. The cancellation rule is available to read on the app.	☐	☐	☐
4. Marci Davis thinks the cancellation fee is too expensive.	☐	☐	☐
5. The company representative apologized for what happened.	☐	☐	☐
6. Marci says ride-sharing agreements should be more clear.	☐	☐	☐

D Have you ever used a ride-sharing service? What do you think of this type of service?

That needs fixing. **41**

Units 5–6 Progress check

SELF-ASSESSMENT

How well can you do these things? Check (✓) the boxes.

I can . . .	Very well	OK	A little
Talk about feelings and expectations (Ex. 1)	☐	☐	☐
Discuss cultural differences (Ex. 2)	☐	☐	☐
Understand problems and complaints (Ex. 3)	☐	☐	☐
Describe problems (Ex. 4)	☐	☐	☐
Discuss what needs to be improved (Ex. 5)	☐	☐	☐

1 SPEAKING Facing new challenges

PAIR WORK Choose a situation. Then ask your partner questions about it using the words in the box. Take turns.

moving to another city   starting a new job
going to a new school   getting married

anxious	excited
curious	insecure
embarrassed	nervous
enthusiastic	worried

A: If you were moving to another city, what would you be nervous about?
B: One thing I'd be nervous about is not having any friends around. I'd be worried about feeling lonely!

2 SURVEY Cultural behavior

A What do you think of these behaviors? Complete the survey.

Is it acceptable to . . . ?	Yes	No	It depends
give money as a gift	☐	☐	☐
call older people by their first names	☐	☐	☐
greet friends with a kiss on the cheek	☐	☐	☐
ask how old someone is	☐	☐	☐
put your feet on the furniture	☐	☐	☐

B **GROUP WORK** Compare your opinions. When are these behaviors acceptable? When are they unacceptable? What behaviors are never acceptable?

A: It's not acceptable to give money as a gift.
B: Oh, I think it depends. I think it's OK to give money to kids and teens, and as a wedding gift, but . . .

3 LISTENING I have a problem.

A Listen to three tenants complain to their building manager. Complete the chart.

	Tenant's complaint	How the problem is solved
1.		
2.		
3.		

B **GROUP WORK** Do you agree with the solutions? How would you solve the problems?

4 ROLE PLAY Haggling

Student A: You want to buy this car from Student B, but it's too expensive. Describe the problems you see to get a better price.

Student B: You are trying to sell this car, but it has some problems. Make excuses for the problems to get the most money.

A: I'm interested in this car, but the door handle is broken. I'll give you $ . . . for it.

B: That's no big deal. You can fix that easily. How about $ . . . ?

A: Well, what about the windshield? It's . . .

B: You can't really see that. . . .

Change roles and try the role play again.

5 DISCUSSION School improvements

A **GROUP WORK** Imagine you are on a school improvement committee. You are discussing changes to your school. Decide on the five biggest issues.

A: The Wi-Fi connection needs to be improved. It keeps disconnecting, and it's not fast enough.

B: Yes, but it's more important to replace the couch in the student lounge. It has a big hole and stains.

B **CLASS ACTIVITY** Share your list with the class. What are the three most needed improvements? Can you think of how to accomplish them?

WHAT'S NEXT?

Look at your Self-assessment again. Do you need to review anything?

Units 5–6 Progress check 43

7 What can we do?

▶ Discuss environmental problems
▶ Compare solutions to social problems

1 SNAPSHOT

WHAT A WASTE!

The United States generates **254 million** tons of waste a year. The average American produces almost **2** kilograms of waste a day.

Fifteen hundred plastic bottles are consumed every second in the United States.
It takes at least **500** years for a plastic bottle to decompose.

Americans throw away around **130 million** cell phones a year. Much of this e-waste ends up in landfills.

In the U.S., **30–40%** of the food supply is wasted. That could feed **millions** of hungry people.

How could we reduce the waste of each of these items?
What do you throw away? What do you tend to recycle?
What are two other environmental problems that concern you?

2 PERSPECTIVES Vote for a better city!

A Listen to an announcement from an election campaign. What kinds of problems does Grace Medina want to fix?

VOTE FOR GRACE MEDINA FOR CITY COUNCIL

Grace Medina's ideas for Riverside!

Have you noticed these problems in our city?
- Our fresh water supply is being contaminated by toxic chemicals.
- The roads aren't being repaired due to a lack of funding.
- Our community center has been closed because of high maintenance costs.
- Our city streets are being damaged as a result of heavy traffic.
- Many public parks have been lost through overbuilding.
- Low-income families are being displaced from their homes due to high rental prices.

GRACE MEDINA – THE CHANGE WE NEED

B Which of these problems affect your city? Can you give specific examples?

3 GRAMMAR FOCUS

Passive with prepositions

Present continuous passive

Our water supply **is being contaminated**	**by** toxic chemicals.
Our city streets **are being damaged**	**as a result of** heavy traffic.
The roads **aren't being repaired**	**due to** a lack of funding.

Present perfect passive

Our community center **has been closed**	**because of** high costs.
Many public parks **have been lost**	**through** overbuilding.

GRAMMAR PLUS see page 138

A **PAIR WORK** Match the photos of environmental problems with the sentences below.

1. High emissions of carbon dioxide are causing climate changes. (by)
2. Rapid urbanization is depleting our natural resources. (through)
3. Water pollution has threatened the health of people all over the world. (due to)
4. Livestock farms have contaminated the soil and underground water. (because of)
5. The destruction of rain forests is accelerating the extinction of plants and wildlife. (as a result of)
6. Oil spills are harming birds, fish, and other marine life. (through)

B Rewrite the sentences in part A using the passive and the prepositions given. Then compare with a partner.

1. *Climate changes are being caused by high emissions of carbon dioxide.*

C **PAIR WORK** Cover the sentences in part A above. Take turns describing the environmental problems in the pictures in your own words.

What can we do? **45**

4 PRONUNCIATION Reduction of auxiliary verbs

A Listen and practice. Notice how the auxiliary verb forms **is**, **are**, **has**, and **have** are reduced in conversation.

Food **is** being wasted.

Streets **are** being damaged.

Our community center **has** been closed.

Parks **have** been lost.

B **PAIR WORK** Practice the sentences you wrote in Exercise 3, part B. Pay attention to the reduction of **is**, **are**, **has**, and **have**.

5 LISTENING Saving the environment

A Listen to three people describe some serious environmental problems. Check (✓) the problem each person talks about.

		Problem		What can be done about it?
1.	Morgan	☐ landfills	☐ poor farmland	
2.	Dalton	☐ electricity	☐ e-waste	
3.	Kendall	☐ air pollution	☐ water pollution	

B Listen again. What can be done to solve each problem? Complete the chart.

C **GROUP WORK** Which problem above worries you the most? What is being done to fix it?

6 WORD POWER Global challenges

A **PAIR WORK** How concerned is your partner about these problems? Check (✓) his or her answers.

Problems	Very concerned	Fairly concerned	Not concerned
unemployment	☐	☐	☐
famine	☐	☐	☐
global warming	☐	☐	☐
government corruption	☐	☐	☐
infectious diseases	☐	☐	☐
political unrest	☐	☐	☐
poverty	☐	☐	☐
recession	☐	☐	☐
violence	☐	☐	☐

B **GROUP WORK** Share your partner's answers with another pair. Which problems concern your group the most? What will happen if the problem isn't solved?

A: Many people have been affected by the high rates of unemployment.
B: We need to create more jobs and invest in education.
C: I agree. If we don't, young people won't have any opportunities in the future.

7 CONVERSATION What if it doesn't work?

A Listen and practice.

Cindy: Did you hear about the dead fish that were found floating in the Bush River this morning?
Otis: Yeah, I read something about it. Do you know what happened?
Cindy: Well, there's a factory outside town that's pumping chemicals into the river.
Otis: How can they do that? Isn't that against the law?
Cindy: Yes, it is. But a lot of companies ignore those laws.
Otis: That's terrible! What can we do about it?
Cindy: Well, one way to change things is to talk to the company's management.
Otis: What if that doesn't work?
Cindy: Well, then another way to stop them is to get a news station to run a story on it.
Otis: Yes! Companies hate bad publicity. By the way, what's the name of this company?
Cindy: Believe it or not, it's called Green Mission Industries.
Otis: Really? My uncle is one of their top executives.

B CLASS ACTIVITY What else could Cindy and Otis do?

C Listen to the rest of the conversation. What do Cindy and Otis decide to do?

8 GRAMMAR FOCUS

Infinitive clauses and phrases

One way **to change** things is	**to talk** to the company's management.
Another way **to stop** them is	**to get** a news station to run a story.
The best ways **to fight** unemployment are	**to create** more jobs and invest in education.

GRAMMAR PLUS see page 138

A Find one or more solutions for each problem. Then compare with a partner.

Problems
1. The best way to fight poverty is _____
2. One way to reduce government corruption is _____
3. One way to reduce unemployment is _____
4. The best way to stop global warming is _____
5. One way to help the homeless is _____
6. One way to improve air quality is _____

Solutions
a. to provide more affordable housing.
b. to create more jobs.
c. to make politicians accountable for decisions.
d. to have more vocational training programs.
e. to increase the use of cleaner energy.
f. to provide education to all children.
g. to build more public shelters.
h. to reduce deforestation.

B GROUP WORK Can you think of two more solutions for each problem in part A? Agree on the best solution for each.

What can we do?

9 DISCUSSION What should be done?

A GROUP WORK Describe the problems shown in the photos. Then make suggestions about how to solve these problems.

What can be done . . . ?
1. to reduce crime
2. to keep our water supplies safe
3. to improve children's health
4. to improve traffic and mobility

A: Our cities are being taken over by criminals.
B: Well, one way to fight crime is to have more police on the streets.
C: That's not enough. The best way to stop it is . . .

B CLASS ACTIVITY Share your solutions. Which ones are the most innovative? Which ones are most likely to solve the problems?

10 INTERCHANGE 7 Take action!

Brainstorm solutions to some local problems. Go to Interchange 7 on page 121.

11 WRITING A post on a community website

A Choose one of the problems from the unit or use one of your own ideas. Write a message to post on a community website.

NO MORE JUNK FOOD!
Our schools are serving poor quality food to our children. School cafeterias offer mostly fast food and soda to students. This has to change. One way to change this is . . .

B PAIR WORK Exchange messages with a partner. Write a response suggesting another solution to his or her problem.

12 READING

A Skim the article. What problem did the island face? What solution did the inhabitants come up with?

Home | News | **Feature stories** | Sign in | Community

TURNING AN INVASION INTO AN ADVANTAGE

Lionfish are beautiful creatures. They are also one of the most invasive and destructive sea creatures on the planet, causing particularly serious problems in the Caribbean Sea. Their numbers have increased dramatically in a few years there, and they have already caused a great deal of damage to the ecosystem.

St. Lucia is a Caribbean island where action is being taken against the invasive species. The island is famous for its clear blue waters, and many tourists enjoy diving in order to explore the wonders of the extensive coral reefs. Unfortunately, lionfish eat the native fish that keep the reefs clean and healthy, putting the reefs at risk. It is estimated that lionfish can eat up to 80% of the small fish in a coral reef in five weeks, and because the invasive fish reproduce very quickly the problem could easily get worse in no time.

Instead of trying to trap or poison the destructive fish, islanders are turning the lionfish invasion to their advantage. They realized that one way to reduce the population of lionfish was to hunt them for sport and business, and then use them for food. Although the fish have a very poisonous sting, they can be prepared so they are safe to eat. And Caribbean cooks were sure to find a way to turn these unwelcome fish into an unforgettable treat.

Unfortunately, the lionfish population has not been reduced by much, but at least the fish have been kept from multiplying too quickly. Jobs have also been provided for unemployed fishermen, who were unable to fish for other types of sea life in the protected waters. The lionfish are still a problem, but the islanders are making the best of a bad situation – and they are making a living from it, too!

B Read the article. Answer the questions.
1. Why are the lionfish a concern?
2. Why is it important to protect the area around St. Lucia?
3. What characteristic makes the lionfish hard to control?
4. What solutions have the islanders come up with?
5. What have the results of the islanders' efforts been?

C **GROUP WORK** What environmental threats exist where you live? Can you think of any creative or unusual ways to deal with them?

What can we do? **49**

8 Never stop learning.

▶ Discuss personal preferences
▶ Discuss ways of learning and life skills

1 SNAPSHOT

Learning: Anywhere, Anytime, for Any Reason

LEARNING PATHS
go to college
take online courses
take traditional training classes
study on your own
set up a study group
attend conferences
watch filmed lectures

LEARNING BENEFITS
get a degree
meet people and expand your network
change jobs or career path
get a raise or promotion at work
get a professional license or certification
learn something that makes your life easier
have fun

Which learning paths have you tried? How was your experience?
Which learning benefits do you consider the most important? Why?
Are you planning to learn anything new this year? What?

2 PERSPECTIVES A survey

A Listen to a survey that a school is conducting about student preferences. Check (✓) the student's answers.

Springfield Center for Continuing Education

New courses survey

1. Would you rather study on your own or join a study group?
   ☐ a. I'd rather study on my own.
   ☐ b. I'd rather join a study group.
   ☐ c. I'd rather do both.

2. Would you rather take an art course or a professional course?
   ☐ a. I'd rather take an art course.
   ☐ b. I'd rather take a professional course.
   ☐ c. I'd rather not take either. I'd rather take a language course.

3. Would you prefer to take an online course or a traditional course?
   ☐ a. I'd prefer to take an online course.
   ☐ b. I'd prefer to take a traditional course.
   ☐ c. I'd prefer not to take either. I'd prefer to hire a private tutor.

B PAIR WORK Take the survey. You can change the underlined information. Discuss your answers with a partner.

3 PRONUNCIATION Intonation in questions of choice

▶ Listen and practice. Notice the intonation in questions of choice.

Would you prefer to study online or at a school?

Would you rather learn something fun or useful?

4 GRAMMAR FOCUS

Would rather and would prefer

Would rather takes the base form of the verb. *Would prefer* usually takes an infinitive. Both are followed by *not* in the negative.

Would you **rather take** an art course or a professional course?
  I'd rather take an art course.
  I'd rather not take either.
  I'd rather take a language course than study art.

Would you prefer to take an online course or a traditional course?
  I'd prefer to take an online course.   **I'd prefer not to take** either.

Let's join a study group.
  I'd rather not join a group.
  I'd rather not.
  I'd prefer not to join a group.
  I'd prefer not to.

GRAMMAR PLUS see page 139

A Complete the conversations with *would* and the appropriate forms of the verbs in parentheses. Then practice with a partner.

1. **A:** _____ you rather _____ (take) a technical course or an art course?
   B: I would prefer _____ (take) an art course. I'd like to learn to paint.

2. **A:** _____ you prefer _____ (get) a promotion or a new job?
   B: Actually, I'm not very happy at my present job, so I'd rather _____ (get) a new job.

3. **A:** _____ you prefer _____ (learn) something fun or something practical?
   B: I guess I'd prefer _____ (study) something practical, like personal finance.

4. **A:** _____ you rather _____ (learn) English in England or Canada?
   B: To tell you the truth, I'd prefer _____ (not study) in either place. I'd rather _____ (go) to Australia because it's warmer there.

5. **A:** If you decided to learn to play an instrument, _____ you prefer _____ (attend) a class or _____ (have) a private tutor?
   B: I'd rather _____ (take) a class than _____ (hire) a tutor.

6. **A:** _____ you rather _____ (have) a job in an office or _____ (work) outdoors?
   B: I'd definitely rather _____ (have) a job where I'm outdoors.

B **PAIR WORK** Take turns asking the questions in part A. Pay attention to intonation. Give your own information when responding.

Never stop learning. **51**

5 LISTENING Do what you love.

A Listen to a conversation between a student and his guidance counselor. Check (✓) the suggestions the guidance counselor gives.

☐ talking to professors   ☐ volunteer work   ☐ more classes
☐ job shadowing   ☐ informational interviews   ☐ internships

B **PAIR WORK** If you could learn more about a job, what job would it be? Why? Which options above would you use?

6 SPEAKING Learn something new

A **GROUP WORK** Think of a personal or professional skill you would like to learn or improve. Discuss how you are planning to learn it. Use the ideas from the Snapshot on page 50, or use your own ideas.

A: I want to speak Italian. I think I'm going to take an online course.
B: It's hard to learn a language online. I think you should go to a language school.
A: I don't know. I'm really shy. I'd rather not have classes with other people.
C: You could . . .

B **CLASS ACTIVITY** Share your ideas with your classmates. Who is going to learn something unusual? How are they going to learn it?

7 INTERCHANGE 8 Making choices

What would you most like to learn? Take a survey. Go to Interchange 8 on page 122.

8 CONVERSATION It works for me.

A Listen and practice.

Marta: So how's your Mandarin class going?
Kevin: Harder than I expected, actually. I'm finding the pronunciation very difficult.
Marta: Well, I imagine it takes a while to get it right. You know, you could improve your accent by watching movies.
Kevin: That's a good idea. But how do you learn new vocabulary? I always seem to forget new words.
Marta: I learn new English words best by writing them down and reviewing them many times. I've been using this vocabulary-building app. It really works for me. Look.
Kevin: Hmm. Maybe I should try something like that!

B Listen to two other students, Rick and Nia, explain how they learn new words. Who uses technology to study? Who organizes words by category?

C **CLASS ACTIVITY** How do you learn new words in a foreign language?

52   Unit 8

9 GRAMMAR FOCUS

> **By + gerund to describe how to do things**
>
> You could improve your accent **by watching** movies.
> I learn new words best **by writing** them down and **reviewing** them many times.
> The best way to learn slang is not **by watching** the news but **by watching** TV series.
>
> **GRAMMAR PLUS** see page 139

A How can you improve your English? Complete the sentences with *by* and the gerund forms of the verbs. Then compare with a partner.

1. A good way to learn idioms is _____ (watch) American sitcoms.
2. The best way to practice what you have learned is _____ (use) it in messages or conversation.
3. Students can become better writers _____ (read) more.
4. You can learn to use grammar correctly _____ (do) grammar exercises online.
5. The best way to develop self-confidence in communication is _____ (talk) with native speakers.
6. You can improve your accent _____ (listen) to songs and singing along.
7. A good way to memorize new vocabulary is _____ (play) vocabulary games.
8. You could become a more fluent reader _____ (read) something you're interested in every day.

B GROUP WORK Complete the sentences in part A with your own ideas. What's the best suggestion for each item?

A: In my opinion, a good way to learn idioms is by talking to native speakers.
B: I think the best way is not by talking to native speakers but by watching TV shows.

10 DISCUSSION Learning styles

A Listen to James and Sophia describe how they developed two skills. How did they learn? Complete the chart.

	James	Sophia
1. become an effective public speaker		
2. learn to drive		

B GROUP WORK How would *you* learn to do the things in the chart?

C GROUP WORK Talk about different ways to learn to do each of these activities. Then agree on the most effective method.

take professional-looking photos
manage your time
cook
become a good conversationalist
break dance
swim
play a musical instrument

Never stop learning. **53**

11 WORD POWER Life skills

A PAIR WORK How do we learn each of these things? Check (✓) your opinions.

	From parents	From school	On our own
communication skills	☐	☐	☐
competitiveness	☐	☐	☐
concern for others	☐	☐	☐
cooperation	☐	☐	☐
creativity	☐	☐	☐
money management	☐	☐	☐
perseverance	☐	☐	☐
problem solving	☐	☐	☐
self-confidence	☐	☐	☐
self-discipline	☐	☐	☐
time management	☐	☐	☐
tolerance	☐	☐	☐

some activities

using a daily planner
volunteering in a hospital
taking a public speaking class
performing in a play
going to museums
learning a martial art
playing a team sport
making a budget

B GROUP WORK How can you develop the skills in part A? Use the activities in the box or your own ideas.

A: You can develop communication skills by taking a public speaking class.
B: You can also develop them by trying to be a better listener.

12 WRITING Something I learned

A Think of a skill you have learned. Read these questions and take notes. Then use your notes to write about what you learned.

What is required to be successful at it?
What are some ways people learn to do it?
How did you learn it?
What was difficult about learning it?

> I used to have serious problems managing my finances, and I never paid my bills on time. I have to admit I had very poor money management skills. Some people learn to manage their money at home or by taking courses at school, but I didn't.
>
> When a friend told me about a personal finance course, I decided to take it. I first learned to keep track of my expenses by recording every penny I spent. Then . . .

B GROUP WORK Share your writing. Have any of your classmates' experiences inspired you to learn a new skill?

54 Unit 8

13 READING

A Have you ever had trouble focusing when you're studying? What did you do about it?

Are you studying the "right" way?

Home | News | Articles | Sign in | Community

You may study differently from your friends, but your study habits are probably not wrong!

Kelly and Maria are best friends with a lot in common. They love doing things together, such as going to movies and concerts, shopping, or just sitting at a local café. Since they take a lot of the same school subjects, they would love to study together, but they find this impossible. Their working styles are so completely different that they can't be in the same room while they are studying!

Kelly would rather study in a clean, open space, whereas Maria works best by surrounding herself with books, papers, and other *clutter*. Kelly prefers to study in a totally silent room, but Maria loves to play music or even have the TV on. Kelly can sit for hours without moving, and often gets all of her homework done in one *sitting*. Maria, on the other hand, is constantly getting up, and claims that she thinks best when she's on the move.

You might be asking yourself, which way of studying gets better results? Many people assume that a silent, uncluttered setting is the way to go, but it seems that is not necessarily the case. Some research has even shown that outside noise and clutter help some people *concentrate* because it makes them form a mental "wall" around what they are doing and improves their focus. So, if you're a student who chooses to study while sitting at a table in a busy shopping mall, don't worry about it. And if you work in total silence, that's OK, too. Judging from Kelly and Maria's study habits, the best way to study is the way that works for you. With their very different *approaches*, both of them do extremely well in school, and both finish their work in about the same amount of time as well.

One curious fact about the two friends: Despite their opposing studying styles, they have almost *identical* ambitions. Both are planning to go to law school – Kelly with the idea of becoming a human rights attorney and Maria hoping to become a public defender. But will they be study buddies? Not a chance!

B Read the article. Find the words in *italics* in the article. Then match each word with its meaning.

1. *clutter* _____
2. *sitting* _____
3. *concentrate* _____
4. *approach* _____
5. *identical* _____

a. focus attention on something
b. exactly the same
c. period of activity without a break
d. way of doing something
e. objects in a state of disorder

C Complete the summary with information from the article. Use one or two words in each blank.

Kelly and Maria are friends who have a lot _____, but they can't study together because they have _____. Kelly likes a _____ that is very quiet, and she can _____ for a long time. Maria prefers a space that is _____, and she likes to _____. Studies show that neither way of studying is _____ than the other. Noise can help some people _____, for example. Despite their different habits, Kelly and Maria are both _____ students, and it is interesting that the friends have _____ plans for the future.

D GROUP WORK Whose studying style is closest to yours, Kelly's or Maria's? Why?

Never stop learning. **55**

Units 7–8 Progress check

SELF-ASSESSMENT

How well can you do these things? Check (✓) the boxes.

I can . . .	Very well	OK	A little
Describe environmental problems (Ex. 1)	☐	☐	☐
Discuss solutions to problems (Ex. 2)	☐	☐	☐
Understand examples of personal qualities (Ex. 3)	☐	☐	☐
Discuss personal preferences (Ex. 4)	☐	☐	☐

1 SPEAKING Environmental issues

PAIR WORK Choose a probable cause for each of the problems and discuss possible solutions.

PROBLEM
- Forests are being destroyed.
- The quality of the air is being lowered.
- Marine life is being affected.
- Water is being contaminated.
- Landfills are overflowing.
- City streets are being damaged.

CAUSE
- the lack of recycling
- heavy traffic
- rapid urbanization
- climate changes
- fumes from cars
- factory waste

A: Forests are being destroyed because of rapid urbanization.
B: We need plans for urban development that don't . . .

2 DISCUSSION Tricky social situations

A PAIR WORK Read these problems that friends sometimes have with each other. Suggest solutions for each problem.

Your friend is always criticizing you and your other friends.
Your best friend never pays for his or her share at group dinners.
A friend is having a party and you weren't invited.

B GROUP WORK Agree on the best solution for each problem.

"The best thing to do is to talk to your friend and say how you feel."

useful expressions

One thing to do is to . . .
Another way to help is to . . .
The best thing to do is . . .

56

3 LISTENING I got it!

A Listen to people talk about recent events and activities in their lives. What events and activities are they talking about? What two qualities does each person's behavior demonstrate? Complete the chart.

a. money management
b. competitiveness
c. creativity
d. concern for others
e. perseverance
f. self-confidence

	Event or activity	Qualities
1. Kate		e,
2. Mark		
3. Iris		

B PAIR WORK Describe a time when you demonstrated one of the qualities above. Can your partner guess the quality?

4 QUESTIONNAIRE Learning styles

A PAIR WORK Interview your partner. Circle the ways your partner prefers to improve his or her English.

1. When you don't understand a word, would you prefer to . . . ?
   a. look it up in a dictionary   or   b. try to guess the meaning
2. If you don't understand what someone says, would you rather . . . ?
   a. ask the person to repeat it   or   b. pretend you understand
3. When you hear a new word in English, would you rather . . . ?
   a. write it down   or   b. try to remember it
4. When you make a mistake in English, would you prefer someone to . . . ?
   a. correct it immediately   or   b. ignore it
5. When you meet a native English speaker, would you prefer to . . . ?
   a. try to talk to the person   or   b. listen while he or she speaks
6. When you have to contact someone in English, would you rather . . . ?
   a. call him or her on the phone   or   b. send him or her an email

"I'd prefer to try to guess the meaning of a new word."

B GROUP WORK Discuss the advantages and disadvantages of each option in part A. Are there better options for each situation?

A: When I try to guess the meaning of a new word, it takes less time, so I can read faster.
B: Yes, but if you look it up, you learn a new word.
C: I think the best way to deal with a new word is to try and guess the meaning, and then check if it makes sense.

WHAT'S NEXT?

Look at your Self-assessment again. Do you need to review anything?

Interchange activities

INTERCHANGE 1 Personality quiz

A PAIR WORK What is your personality type? Take turns using the quiz to interview each other. Then tally your answers and find out which category best describes you.

What's your personality type?

1. **When you fail a test, do you:**
   a. get really upset and decide to try much harder next time?
   b. go over your answers and learn from your mistakes?
   c. not care much about it?

2. **When you work on a big project, do you:**
   a. try to finish it as quickly as possible?
   b. work at it over a long period of time?
   c. put it off as long as possible?

3. **When you do an assignment, do you:**
   a. try to do a first-class job so people will notice?
   b. do it as well as you can without worrying too much?
   c. do only what you must to get it done?

4. **When faced with a difficult challenge, do you:**
   a. look forward to facing it?
   b. worry about dealing with it?
   c. try to avoid it?

5. **Do you think the best way to get the most out of a day is to:**
   a. do as many things as possible?
   b. take your time to get things done?
   c. do only those things you really have to?

6. **When something doesn't work out the way you want it to, do you:**
   a. get angry with yourself and others?
   b. think calmly about what to do next?
   c. give up, because it wasn't important anyway?

7. **When people take a long time to finish something, do you:**
   a. get impatient and do it yourself?
   b. gently ask them to do it more quickly?
   c. let them take their time?

8. **When you are learning a new skill, do you:**
   a. work very hard to master it quickly?
   b. do your best and often ask for help?
   c. take your time and enjoy the learning experience?

9. **If you compare your goals with your friends' goals, do you:**
   a. want to accomplish greater things than they do?
   b. hope to achieve similar things in life?
   c. not care if they set higher goals for themselves than you do?

10. **When people are late for appointments, do you:**
    a. get angry and stressed out?
    b. remember that you are sometimes late, too?
    c. not worry, because you are usually late, too?

11. **When people are talking to you, do you:**
    a. not listen and think about other things?
    b. listen and participate in the conversation?
    c. let them talk and agree with everything they say?

Scoring
Count how many a, b, and c answers your partner has. If there are . . .

mostly a answers: This person is a high achiever but can get very stressed.

mostly b answers: This person is the cool and steady type.

mostly c answers: This person is the easygoing or carefree type.

B GROUP WORK Compare your scores. Then suggest four characteristics of each personality type.

"A high achiever is the kind of person who . . . . He or she can't stand it when . . ."

INTERCHANGE 2 Networking

A PAIR WORK Imagine you and your partner are organizing a dinner party for new entrepreneurs and potential investors.

Read about each person on the guest list.

| Home | About | News | **Business** | Community | Sign in |

ENTREPRENEURS

Gaston Lafont is 25, single, and a promising chef. He's friendly and ambitious, but he can be very moody. He's coming to the party to get celebrities and powerful business executives to invest in his restaurant.

Melissa Dominguez is 28, single, and a computer wizard. She puts her career ahead of her personal life and has few interests apart from her work. She needs funding for a new start-up company.

Don Hart is 32, married, and an environmentalist. He's egotistical, outspoken, and tends to start arguments. He wants to run for mayor and needs funding for his campaign.

Emma Stewart is 30, single, and a medical researcher. She's shy and introverted and has devoted her life to helping children around the world. She's currently developing a new vaccine for a widespread tropical disease.

INVESTORS

Mike Hunter is 54, a widower, and an oil tycoon. This millionaire is bossy and straightforward. His companies have been accused of destroying the environment in many countries.

Paola Di Matteo is 23, single, and a world-famous movie star. She's very private about her personal life, and she is interested in investing in young talent.

Joanne Parson is 42, single, and an art and nature lover. Wealthy and sociable, she takes part in several volunteer projects and gives substantial amounts of money to various causes around the world.

Ren Okawa is 38, married, and a stockbroker. He likes to invest in new companies and has helped many startups and young entrepreneurs succeed. He's smart, ambitious, and has sophisticated taste in art and food.

B PAIR WORK Discuss the possible seating arrangements for the party. Then complete this seating plan.

A: Let's seat Gaston next to Ren. Gaston is interested in finding investors for his new restaurant.

B: It might be better to put Ren next to Melissa. Ren likes to invest in start-ups, so . . .

Interchange 2

INTERCHANGE 3   Beg and borrow

A Imagine you own these items. Which ones would you be willing to lend to a friend? Which ones wouldn't you lend? Check (✓) a response for each item.

TENT
☐ wouldn't mind lending
☐ wouldn't want to lend

TABLET
☐ wouldn't mind lending
☐ wouldn't want to lend

CAR
☐ wouldn't mind lending
☐ wouldn't want to lend

MOUNTAIN BIKE
☐ wouldn't mind lending
☐ wouldn't want to lend

POWER DRILL
☐ wouldn't mind lending
☐ wouldn't want to lend

CLASS NOTES
☐ wouldn't mind lending
☐ wouldn't want to lend

CAMERA
☐ wouldn't mind lending
☐ wouldn't want to lend

SLEEPING BAG
☐ wouldn't mind lending
☐ wouldn't want to lend

HEADPHONES
☐ wouldn't mind lending
☐ wouldn't want to lend

B **CLASS ACTIVITY** Go around the class and take turns asking to borrow each item in part A. Explain why you want to borrow it. When responding, say if you are willing to lend the item or not. If you won't lend something, say why.

A: Would you mind lending me your tent for the weekend? I want to go camping, but I got a hole in my tent.
B: I'm sorry, but I don't think I can. I might want to go camping this weekend, too!
OR
B: Sure. Just come over tonight and pick it up.

C **CLASS ACTIVITY** Who was able to borrow the most items?

INTERCHANGE 4 Spin a yarn

A GROUP WORK Place a pen on the CHARACTER spinner and spin it. Repeat for the other two spinners. Use the elements the pen points at to create a story. If the pen points at YOU DECIDE, you can use any element from that spinner, or you can invent a new one.

CHARACTER
- a young woman
- a child
- a clumsy man
- YOU DECIDE
- a teenager
- an elderly lady

SETTING
- on the street
- in a park
- at the mall
- YOU DECIDE
- at a restaurant
- at a party

EVENT
- mishap
- emergency
- triumph
- YOU DECIDE
- coincidence
- lucky break

"One day a clumsy man was having dinner at a restaurant when . . ."

B CLASS ACTIVITY Share your group's stories with your classmates. Who created the most interesting story? the most unexpected? the most creative?

Interchange 4

INTERCHANGE 5 Cultural dos and taboos

A These statements are generally true about cultural behavior in the United States. Check (✓) those that are true in your country.

COMPARING CULTURES
Find out how typical U.S. cultural behavior compares to yours!

SOCIALIZING AND ENTERTAINING

☐ 1. It's OK to start a conversation with a stranger when waiting in line.
☐ 2. People aren't supposed to stand too close to other people when talking.
☐ 3. In general, people wear outdoor shoes inside their homes.
☐ 4. Women often hug their female friends when they meet.
☐ 5. It's not acceptable to ask people how much money they earn or how much they paid for things.
☐ 6. People are expected to call or text before dropping by a friend's house.
☐ 7. When invited to someone's home for dinner, people usually arrive on time.
☐ 8. Gifts are normally opened when received.

DINING AND SHOPPING

☐ 9. It's acceptable to eat while walking outside.
☐ 10. Eating is not allowed while shopping in most stores.
☐ 11. When eating in a restaurant, friends either split the cost of the meal or take turns paying.
☐ 12. It's the custom to leave a 15–20% tip for the server at a restaurant.
☐ 13. It's uncommon to bargain when you buy things in stores.

AT WORK AND SCHOOL

☐ 14. In an office, people usually prefer to be called by their first names.
☐ 15. Students remain seated when the teacher enters the classroom.

DATING AND MARRIAGE

☐ 16. It's acceptable for most teenagers to go out on dates.
☐ 17. People usually decide for themselves who they will marry.

B **PAIR WORK** Compare your answers with a partner. For the statements you didn't check, why do you think these behaviors are different in your country?

INTERCHANGE 6A Home makeover

Student A

A Look at this apartment. What's wrong with it? First, make a list of as many problems as you can find in each room.

B PAIR WORK Compare your lists. What are the similarities and differences in the problems between your picture and your partner's picture? Ask questions to find the differences.

A: What's wrong in the bedroom?
B: Well, in my picture, the walls need painting. And the curtains . . .
A: Oh, really? In my picture, the walls need to be painted, but the curtains . . . , and the window . . .

Interchange 6a 119

INTERCHANGE 6B Home makeover

Student B

A Look at this apartment. What's wrong with it? First, make a list of as many problems as you can find in each room.

B PAIR WORK Compare your lists. What are the similarities and differences in the problems between your picture and your partner's picture? Ask questions to find the differences.

A: What's wrong in the bedroom?
B: Well, in my picture, the walls need painting. And the curtains . . .
A: Oh, really? In my picture, the walls need to be painted, but the curtains . . . , and the window . . .

Interchange 6b

INTERCHANGE 7 Take action!

A Read about these issues. Which one would you most likely protest?

> A baby food company has been using genetically modified fruit and vegetables in their recipes to lower costs.

> Congress is discussing a law that allows the government to shut down any website it considers inappropriate.

> The city is going to close a public park to build a new bus terminal.

B GROUP WORK Find other students who chose the same issue. Then look at methods of protest. Which are the most effective for the issue you chose? Complete the chart.

METHOD OF PROTEST	VERY EFFECTIVE	SOMEWHAT EFFECTIVE	NOT EFFECTIVE
start an online campaign	☐	☐	☐
stage a sit-in	☐	☐	☐
organize a demonstration	☐	☐	☐
boycott a product or service	☐	☐	☐
ask people to sign an online petition	☐	☐	☐
contact local news stations	☐	☐	☐
contact your local government representative	☐	☐	☐
distribute pamphlets about the issue	☐	☐	☐
hold an awareness campaign in the community	☐	☐	☐
create posters and signs to hang up around town	☐	☐	☐

Develop a strategy to make your voices heard using the above methods or your own ideas.

C CLASS ACTIVITY How did you decide to deal with the issue? Present your group's strategy to the class.

Interchange 7

INTERCHANGE 8 Making choices

A Complete this chart with information about yourself. Add one idea of your own.

two artistic skills I'd like to develop	_____	_____
two adventurous activities I'd like to try	_____	_____
two dances I'd like to learn	_____	_____
two topics I'd like to learn more about	_____	_____
two foreign languages I'd like to speak	_____	_____
two dishes I'd like to learn how to cook	_____	_____
two volunteer activities I'd like to do	_____	_____
two courses I'd like to take	_____	_____
two sports I'd like to play	_____	_____
two skills I'd like to improve	_____	_____
two _____	_____	_____

B **CLASS ACTIVITY** Ask three classmates to help you choose between the things you wrote down in part A. Write their recommendations in the chart.

Names:	_____	_____	_____
artistic skill			
adventurous activity			
dance			
topic			
foreign language			
dish			
volunteer activity			
course			
sport			
skill			
_____			

A: I don't know if I'd rather be a graffiti artist or a painter. What do you think?
B: Hmm. If I were you, I'd choose graffiti.
A: Why graffiti and not painting?
B: Well, that kind of street art is very popular nowadays. You could become famous, and . . .

C **GROUP WORK** What are your final choices? Who gave the best advice? Why?

Interchange 8

This page is intentionally left blank

Grammar plus

UNIT 1

1 Relative pronouns — page 3

- A relative pronoun – *who* or *that* – is necessary when the pronoun is the subject of the clause: I'd love to meet someone **who/that** is considerate. (NOT: I'd love to meet ~~someone is considerate~~.)
- When the pronoun is the object of the clause, *who* and *that* can be left out: I'd like a roommate **who/that** I have a lot in common with. OR I'd like a roommate I have a lot in common with.

Complete the conversation with *who* or *that*. Put an ✗ when a relative pronoun isn't necessary.

A: Ana, have you met Clint – the guy ___✗___ Laurie is going to marry?
B: Oh, Clint and I have been friends for years. In fact, I'm the one _____ introduced Laurie and Clint.
A: Do you think they're right for each other?
B: Definitely. They're two people _____ have a lot in common – but not *too* much.
A: What does that mean?
B: Well, you don't want a partner _____ doesn't have his or her own interests. Couples _____ do everything together usually don't last very long.
A: I guess you're right, but the opposite isn't good, either. My last girlfriend was someone _____ I had nothing in common with. She wasn't the kind of girl _____ I could talk to easily.
B: Well, you can talk to *me* easily. . . .

2 *It* clauses + adverbial clauses with *when* — page 6

- In sentences with an *it* clause + an adverbial clause with *when*, the word *it* refers to and means the same as the adverbial clause with *when*. The *it* in these sentences is necessary and cannot be left out: I hate **it when** people talk on a cell phone in an elevator. (NOT: ~~I hate when~~ people . . .) **It** bothers me **when** people talk on a cell phone in an elevator. (NOT: ~~Bothers~~ me when people . . .)

Rewrite the sentences using the words in parentheses.

1. I can't stand it when people call me before 8:00 A.M. (it really bothers me)
   It really bothers me when people call me before 8:00 a.m.

2. It upsets me when I don't have enough time to study for an exam. (I hate it)
   _____

3. I don't mind it when friends talk to me about their problems. (it doesn't bother me)
   _____

4. I don't like it when I forget a co-worker's name. (it embarrasses me)
   _____

5. It makes me happy when my friends send me videos. (I love it)
   _____

6. I hate it when I have to wait for someone. (it upsets me)
   _____

UNIT 2

1 Gerund phrases — page 9

- A gerund phrase as a subject takes a singular verb: Taking care of children **is** a rewarding job. (NOT: Taking care of children ~~are~~ a rewarding job.)
- There are some common verb + preposition expressions (for example, *dream about, feel like, talk about, think about*) and adjective + preposition phrases (for example, *good/bad at, excited by/about, interested in, tired of, used to*) that are followed by a gerund: I'm **thinking about looking for** a new job. I'm **tired of working** long hours.

Complete the sentences with the correct gerund forms of the verbs in the box.

✓ become	have	make	stand	travel
change	learn	solve	take	work

1. My brother's very interested in _____becoming_____ a flight attendant. He dreams about _____ to new places.
2. I'm excited about _____ a Japanese class next semester. I enjoy _____ languages.
3. You wouldn't like _____ in a restaurant. You'd get tired of _____ on your feet throughout the long shifts!
4. Our teacher is very good at _____ problems. Maybe she should think about _____ careers to become a guidance counselor.
5. _____ a living as a photographer could be challenging. _____ an impressive portfolio is really important to attract new clients and employers.

2 Comparisons — page 11

- When making general comparisons with count nouns, use *a/an* + singular noun or no article + plural noun: **A pilot** earns more than **a flight attendant**. **Pilots** earn more than **flight attendants**. (NOT: ~~The~~ pilots earn more than ~~the~~ flight attendants.)

Make comparisons with the information below. Add articles and other words when necessary.

1. architect / more education / hairstylist
   An architect needs more education than a hairstylist.
2. college professor / earn more / elementary school teacher
   _____
3. nurses / worse hours / psychiatrists
   _____
4. working as a police officer / as dangerous / being a firefighter
   _____
5. taxi driver / not as well paid / electrician
   _____
6. being a tour guide / less interesting / being an actor
   _____

Unit 2 Grammar plus 133

UNIT 3

1 Requests with modals, *if* clauses, and gerunds   page 17

■ Use the simple past form – not the gerund or simple present form – after *if* with *Would you mind . . . ?* and *Would it be all right . . . ?*: **Would you mind if I used** your car? **Would it be all right if I used** your car? (NOT: Would you mind if I ~~using~~ your car? OR Would it be all right if I ~~use~~ your car?)

Read the situations. Then complete the requests.

1. You want to borrow a friend's underwater camera for a diving trip.
   A: I was wondering if *I could borrow your underwater camera.*
   B: Sure. That's fine. Just please be careful with it.
2. You want to use your roommate's computer.
   A: Is it OK _____
   B: You can use it, but please don't drink near it.
3. Your neighbor has a car. You need a ride to class.
   A: Would you mind _____
   B: I'd be glad to. What time should I pick you up?
4. You want your brother to help you move on Saturday.
   A: Can you _____
   B: I'm sorry. I'm busy all weekend.
5. You would like a second piece of your aunt's cherry pie.
   A: Would it be all right _____
   B: Yes, of course! Just pass me your plate.
6. You want to borrow your cousin's red sweater.
   A: Could you _____
   B: Sorry. I don't like it when other people wear my clothes.

2 Indirect requests   page 20

■ In indirect requests with negative infinitives, *not* comes before – not between – the infinitive: Could you tell Allie **not to be** late? (NOT: Could you tell Allie ~~to not be~~ late?)

Complete the indirect requests. Ask someone to deliver the messages to Susie.

1. Are you busy this weekend?   →   Could *you ask Susie if she's busy this weekend?*
2. Do you want to hang out with me?   →   Can _____
3. Text me.   →   Can _____
4. Do you know my address?   →   Can _____
5. Don't forget to write.   →   Could _____
6. What are you doing Saturday?   →   Can _____
7. Do you have plans on Sunday?   →   Could _____

134 Unit 3 Grammar plus

UNIT 4

1 Past continuous vs. simple past — page 23

- Verbs for non-actions or states are rarely used in the past continuous: I **wanted** to stop, but I couldn't. (NOT: I ~~was wanting~~ to stop . . .)

Circle the best forms to complete the conversations.

1. **A:** How **did you break** / **were you breaking** your arm?
   B: It's a crazy story! Ramon and I **rode** / **were riding** our bikes in the park when a cat **ran** / **was running** out in front of me. I **went** / **was going** pretty fast, so when I **tried** / **was trying** to stop, I **went** / **was going** off the road and **fell** / **was falling**.
   A: That's terrible! **Did you go** / **Were you going to** the hospital after it **happened** / **was happening**?
   B: Yes. Luckily, we **weren't** / **weren't being** too far from City Hospital, so we **went** / **were going** there.

2. **A:** You'll never guess what **happened** / **was happening** to me this morning!
   B: What?
   A: Well, I **brushed** / **was brushing** my teeth when suddenly the water **went** / **was going** off. I **had** / **was having** toothpaste all over my mouth, and I couldn't wash it off.
   B: So what **did you do** / **were you doing**?
   A: Fortunately, I **had** / **was having** a big bottle of water in the refrigerator, so I **used** / **was using** that water to rinse my mouth.

2 Past perfect — page 25

- Use the past perfect to show that one past action happened before another past action:
  I **wasn't able to** pay for lunch because I **had left** my wallet at work.

  PAST ——————— X ——————————— X ——— NOW
             had left my wallet   wasn't able to pay

Combine the two ideas into one with a past event and a past perfect event. Use *when* or *because*.

1. The museum closed. A thief stole a famous painting earlier.
   <u>The museum closed because a thief had stolen a famous painting earlier.</u>

2. We finished cleaning the house. Then our guests arrived.
   _____

3. Someone robbed my house yesterday. I left the window open.
   _____

4. There was no food in the house. We forgot to stop at the supermarket.
   _____

5. I called her three times. She finally answered.
   _____

6. I knew about the problem. Your brother told me about it.
   _____

Unit 4 Grammar plus **135**

UNIT 5

1 Noun phrases containing relative clauses — page 31

> ■ The relative pronoun *who* or *that* can be left out in noun phrases as subjects and as objects. These four sentences have exactly the same meaning: One thing I'd be nervous about is getting lost. One thing that I'd be nervous about is getting lost. Getting lost is one thing I'd be nervous about. Getting lost is one thing that I'd be nervous about.

Answer the questions using the words in parentheses. Write each sentence two ways. Leave out the relative pronouns.

If you went to live in a foreign country, . . .

1. Who would you miss a lot? (person: my best friend)
   a. One person I'd miss a lot is my best friend.
   b. My best friend is one person I'd miss a lot.
2. What would you be very interested in? (things: the food and the music)
   a. _____
   b. _____
3. What would you be worried about? (something: not understanding the customs)
   a. _____
   b. _____
4. Who would you stay in touch with? (people: my brother and sister)
   a. _____
   b. _____
5. What would you feel insecure about? (thing: speaking a new language)
   a. _____
   b. _____

2 Expectations — page 33

> ■ Use the base form of a verb – not the gerund – after these expressions for expectations: *be the custom to, be supposed to, be expected to, be acceptable to*: It's the custom to **arrive** a little late. (NOT: It's the custom to ~~arriving~~ a little late.)

Complete the sentences with the clauses in the box.

> it's not acceptable to show up without calling first.
> it's the custom for them to sit across from each other.
> you're expected to reply within a few days.
> you're supposed to bring a gift.
> ✓ you're supposed to shake his or her hand.

1. When you meet someone for the first time, you're supposed to shake his or her hand.
2. When a friend sends you an email, _____
3. If you want to visit someone, _____
4. If you invite a married couple to dinner, _____
5. When you go to a birthday party, _____

UNIT 6

1 Describing problems 1 — page 37

> ■ The simple past and the past participle of regular verbs are the same: I **chipped** the vase. The vase is **chipped**. BUT Many irregular verbs have different simple past and past participle forms: I **tore** my jacket. My jacket is **torn**.

Complete the conversations with the correct words from the box.

are stained	has a dent	✓ have a tear	is broken	is scratched
has a chip	has a stain	is a hole	is leaking	some damage

1. **A:** Oh, no! These jeans ____have a tear____ in them.
   B: And they _____, too.
2. **A:** This table has _____ on top.
   B: I know. The wood _____ because my son drags his toy cars on it.
3. **A:** Why are you drinking out of that glass? It _____ in it.
   B: Oh, I didn't see it. That's why it _____.
4. **A:** Someone hit my car today. Look! The door _____ in it.
   B: I see that. Your back light _____, too.
5. **A:** I bought this blouse yesterday, but I have to take it back. There _____ in it.
   B: It's really cute, but that's not the only problem. It _____ on it, too.

2 Describing problems 2 — page 39

> ■ Use the past participle – not the present participle or gerund – with passive forms:
> The oven needs to be **fixed**. (NOT: The oven needs to be ~~fixing~~.)

A Complete the conversation with the verbs in parentheses.
Use *need* + passive infinitive in A's lines and *need* + gerund in B's lines.

A: Look at this place! A lot of work ____needs to be done____ (do) before we move in.
B: You're not kidding. Let's make a list. First, the walls ____need painting____ (paint).
A: Right. And the windows _____ (wash). Add the rug to your list:
It really _____ (clean). Do you think it _____ (dry-clean)?
B: No, I think we can do it ourselves. It _____ (shampoo).
We can rent a machine for that.
A: And what about the ceiling fan? I think it _____ (replace).
Fans aren't too expensive.
B: OK. I've added it to the list. And what should we do with all this old furniture?
A: It _____ (throw out)! I think the landlord should take care of that, though.

B Complete the blog with the correct form of *keep* and the verb in parentheses.

I ____keep having____ (have) technical problems. My computer _____ (crash),
and my printer _____ (jam). I have to _____ (put) a new
battery into my mouse because it _____ (die). The letters on my keyboard
_____ (stick), too. I _____ (think) things will get better,
but they just _____ (get) worse. Time for some new electronics!

Unit 6 Grammar plus **137**

UNIT 7

1 Passive with prepositions — page 45

■ The prepositions *by*, *as a result of*, *because of*, *though*, and *due to* have similar meanings. They are used in sentences that describe cause and effect; they introduce the cause.

Match phrases from each column to make sentences. (More than one answer may be possible.)

Subject	Effect	Cause
1. The environment	is being contaminated due to	improper disposal of medical waste.
2. Our soil	is being harmed by	deforestation to make paper products.
3. Infectious diseases	are being endangered due to	hybrid cars.
4. Many different species	has been affected because of	the use of pesticides on fruits and vegetables.
5. Our air quality	has been reduced as a result of	the destruction of their habitats.
6. Smog pollution	have been spread through	climate changes like global warming.

2 Infinitive clauses and phrases — page 47

■ The form of *be* that follows the first infinitive must agree with the subject:
The best way to reduce pollution **is** to improve public transportation.
BUT The best ways to reduce homelessness **are** to build more public housing and provide free health care.

A Match the phrases.

1. What are the best ways to make __e__
2. And the best way to do that is _____
3. The best ways to reduce _____
4. One way to improve _____
5. Another way to make _____

a. people safer is to make the air healthier.
b. to create a larger police force.
c. people's quality of life is to help them feel safe.
d. air pollution are to ban cars and control industry.
e. this city a better place to live?

B Complete the conversation with the sentences above.

A: <u>What are the best ways to make this city a better place to live?</u>
B: Well, _____
A: That's right. _____ _____
B: I agree. _____
A: Yes. Good air quality is key. _____
B: Maybe it's time to share our ideas with the mayor. Get out your phone.

UNIT 8

1 Would rather and would prefer — page 51

- In negative statements with *would rather* and *would prefer*, the word *not* comes after the verbs: I'**d rather not**/I'**d prefer not** to take any courses this semester. (NOT: I wouldn't rather/I wouldn't prefer to . . .)

Write questions and responses using the words in parentheses.

1. A: <u>Would you prefer to take classes during the day or at night?</u>
   (prefer / take classes / during the day / at night)
   B: _____
   (rather / take classes / at night)
2. A: _____
   (rather / study / business / education)
   B: _____
   (prefer / become / a teacher)
3. A: _____
   (prefer / sign up for / an art course / a computer course)
   B: _____
   (prefer / not / take / any classes this semester)
4. A: _____
   (rather / take up / an individual sport / a team sport)
   B: _____
   (rather / not / take up / either)

2 By + gerund to describe how to do things — page 53

- In negative sentences that express comparison with *by* + gerund and *but*, *not* comes before *by*: A good way to improve your accent is **not by watching** TV **but by talking** to native speakers. In negative sentences with *by* that give advice without a comparison, *not* comes after *by*: A good way to improve your accent is **by not imitating** non-native speakers.

Combine the two ideas into one sentence using *by* + gerund.

1. You can build your vocabulary. Write down new words and expressions.
   <u>One way to build your vocabulary is by writing down new words and expressions.</u>
2. There is a good way to improve your accent. You can mimic native speakers.
   _____
3. Students can improve their listening skills. They can listen to English-language podcasts.
   _____
4. Hardworking students improve their grammar. They don't repeat common mistakes.
   _____
5. You can become fluent. Don't translate everything. Try to think in English.
   _____
6. You can become a good conversationalist. Don't just talk with others. Talk to yourself when you're alone, too.
   _____

Unit 8 Grammar plus 139

Grammar plus answer key

Unit 1
1 Relative pronouns
A: Ana, have you met Clint – the guy **X** Laurie is going to marry?
B: Oh, Clint and I have been friends for years. In fact, I'm the one **who/that** introduced Laurie and Clint.
A: Do you think they're right for each other?
B: Definitely. They're two people **who/that** have a lot in common – but not *too* much.
A: What does that mean?
B: Well, you don't want a partner **who/that** doesn't have his or her own interests. Couples **who/that** do everything together usually don't last very long.
A: I guess you're right, but the opposite isn't good, either. My last girlfriend was someone **X** I had nothing in common with. She wasn't the kind of girl **X** I could talk to easily.
B: Well, you can talk to *me* easily. . . .

2 *It* clauses + adverbial clauses with *when*
2. I hate it when I don't have enough time to study for an exam.
3. It doesn't bother me when friends talk to me about their problems.
4. It embarrasses me when I forget a co-worker's name.
5. I love it when my friends send me videos.
6. It upsets me when I have to wait for someone.

Unit 2
1 Gerund phrases
1. My brother's very interested in **becoming** a flight attendant. He dreams about **traveling** to new places.
2. I'm excited about **taking** a Japanese class next semester. I enjoy **learning** languages.
3. You wouldn't like **working** in a restaurant. You'd get tired of **standing** on your feet throughout the long shifts!
4. Our teacher is very good at **solving** problems. Maybe she should think about **changing** careers to become a guidance counselor.
5. **Making** a living as a photographer could be challenging. **Having** an impressive portfolio is really important to attract new clients and employers.

2 Comparisons
Answers may vary. Some possible answers:
2. A college professor earns more than an elementary school teacher.
3. Nurses have worse hours than psychiatrists.
4. Working as a police officer is as dangerous as being a firefighter.
5. A taxi driver isn't as well paid as an electrician.
6. Being a tour guide is less interesting than being an actor.

Unit 3
1 Requests with modals, *if* clauses, and gerunds
Answers may vary. Some possible answers:
2. A: Is it OK **if I use your computer?**
   B: You can use it, but please don't drink near it.
3. A: Would you mind **giving me a ride to class?**
   B: I'd be glad to. What time should I pick you up?
4. A: Can you **help me move on Saturday?**
   B: I'm sorry. I'm busy all weekend.
5. A: Would it be all right **if I had another piece of pie?**
   B: Yes, of course! Just pass me your plate.
6. A: Could you **lend me your red sweater?**
   B: Sorry. I don't like it when other people wear my clothes.

2 Indirect requests
2. Can you ask Susie if she wants to hang out with me?
3. Can you ask/tell Susie to text me?
4. Can you ask Susie if she knows my address?
5. Could you tell Susie not to forget to write?
6. Can you ask Susie what she's doing on Saturday?
7. Could you ask Susie if she has plans on Sunday?

Unit 4
1 Past continuous vs. simple past
1. A: How **did you break** your arm?
   B: It's a crazy story! Ramon and I **were riding** our bikes in the park when a cat **ran** out in front of me. I **was going** pretty fast, so when I **tried** to stop, I **went** off the road and **fell**.
   A: That's terrible! **Did you go** to the hospital after it **happened**?
   B: Yes. Luckily, we **weren't** too far from City Hospital, so we **went** there.
2. A: You'll never guess what **happened** to me this morning!
   B: What?
   A: Well, I **was brushing** my teeth when suddenly the water **went** off. I **had** toothpaste all over my mouth, and I couldn't wash it off.
   B: So what **did you do**?
   A: Fortunately, I **had** a big bottle of water in the refrigerator, so I **used** that water to rinse my mouth.

2 Past perfect
2. We had finished cleaning the house when our guests arrived.
3. Someone robbed my house yesterday because I had left the window open.
4. There was no food in the house because we had forgotten to stop at the supermarket.
5. I had called her three times when she finally answered.
6. I knew about the problem because your brother had told me about it.

Unit 5

1 Noun phrases containing relative clauses
2. a. Two things (that) I'd be very interested in are the food and the music.
   b. The food and the music are two things (that) I'd be very interested in.
3. a. Something (that) I'd be worried about is not understanding the customs.
   b. Not understanding the customs is something (that) I'd be worried about.
4. a. Two people (who/that) I'd stay in touch with are my brother and sister.
   b. My brother and sister are two people (who/that) I'd stay in touch with.
5. a. One thing (that) I'd feel insecure about is speaking a new language.
   b. Speaking a new language is one thing (that) I'd feel insecure about.

2 Expectations
2. When a friend sends you an email, **you're expected to reply within a few days.**
3. If you want to visit someone, **it's not acceptable to show up without calling first.**
4. If you invite a married couple to dinner, **it's the custom for them to sit across from each other.**
5. When you go to a birthday party, **you're supposed to bring a gift.**

Unit 6

1 Describing problems 1
1. A: Oh, no! These jeans **have a tear** in them.
   B: And they **are stained**, too.
2. A: This table has **some damage** on top.
   B: I know. The wood **is scratched** because my son drags his toy cars on it.
3. A: Why are you drinking out of that glass? It **has a chip** in it.
   B: Oh, I didn't see it. That's why it **is leaking**.
4. A: Someone hit my car today. Look! The door **has a dent** in it.
   B: I see that. Your back light **is broken**, too.
5. A: I bought this blouse yesterday, but I have to take it back. There **is a hole** in it.
   B: It's really cute, but that's not the only problem. It **has a stain** on it, too.

2 Describing problems 2
A
A: Look at this place! A lot of work **needs to be done** before we move in.
B: You're not kidding. Let's make a list. First, the walls **need painting**.
A: Right. And the windows **need to be washed**. Add the rug to your list: It really **needs to be cleaned**. Do you think it **needs to be dry-cleaned**?
B: No, I think we can do it ourselves. It **needs shampooing**. We can rent a machine for that.
A: And what about the ceiling fan? I think it **needs to be replaced**. Fans aren't too expensive.
B: OK. I've added it to the list. And what should we do with all this old furniture?
A: It **needs to be thrown out**! I think the landlord should take care of that, though.

B
I **keep having** technical problems. My computer **keeps crashing**, and my printer **keeps jamming**. I have to **keep putting** a new battery into my mouse because it **keeps dying**. The letters on my keyboard **keep sticking**, too. I **keep thinking** things will get better, but they just **keep getting** worse. Time for some new electronics!

Unit 7

1 Passive with prepositions
Answers may vary. Some possible answers:
2. Our soil is being contaminated due to the use of pesticides on fruits and vegetables.
3. Infectious diseases have been spread through improper disposal of medical waste.
4. Many different species are being endangered due to the destruction of their habitats.
5. Our air quality has been affected because of deforestation to make paper products.
6. Smog pollution has been reduced as a result of hybrid cars.

2 Infinitive clauses and phrases
A
2. b   3. d   4. c   5. a
B
B: Well, **one way to improve people's quality of life is to help them feel safe.**
A: That's right. **And the best way to do that is to create a larger police force.**
B: I agree. **Another way to make people safer is to make the air healthier.**
A: Yes. Good air quality is key. **The best ways to reduce air pollution are to ban cars and control industry.**
B: Maybe it's time to share our ideas with the mayor. Get out your phone.

Unit 8

1 Would rather and would prefer
1. A: Would you prefer to take classes during the day or at night?
   B: I'd rather take classes at night.
2. A: Would you rather study business or education?
   B: I'd prefer to become a teacher.
3. A: Would you prefer to sign up for an art course or a computer course?
   B: I'd prefer not take any classes this semester.
4. A: Would you rather take up an individual sport or a team sport?
   B: I'd rather not take up either.

2 By + gerund to describe how to do things
2. A good way to improve your accent is by mimicking native speakers.
3. Students can improve their listening skills by listening to English-language podcasts.
4. Hardworking students improve their grammar by not repeating common mistakes.
5. You can become fluent not by translating everything but by trying to think in English.
6. You can become a good conversationalist not just by talking with others but by talking to yourself when you're alone, too.

Grammar plus answer key 149

Credits

The authors and publishers acknowledge the following sources of copyright material and are grateful for the permissions granted. While every effort has been made, it has not always been possible to identify the sources of all the material used, or to trace all copyright holders. If any omissions are brought to our notice, we will be happy to include the appropriate acknowledgements on reprinting and in the next update to the digital edition, as applicable.

Key: Ex = Exercise, T = Top, B = Below, C = Centre,
TR = Top Right, BR = Below Right, TL = Top Left, TC = Top Centre,
BL = Below Left, BC = Below Centre, L = Left, R = Right,
CL = Centre Left, B/G = Background.

Illustrations
Mark Duffin: 39, 115, 119, 120; Thomas Girard (Good Illustration): 86; Dusan Lakicevic (Beehive Illustration): 18, 24; Gavin Reece (New Division): 43.

Photos
Back cover (woman with whiteboard): Jenny Acheson/Stockbyte/GettyImages; Back cover (whiteboard): Nemida/GettyImages; Back cover (man using phone): Betsie Van Der Meer/Taxi/GettyImages; Back cover (woman smiling): PeopleImages.com/DigitalVision/GettyImages; Back cover (name tag): Tetra Images/GettyImages; Back cover (handshake): David Lees/Taxi/GettyImages; p. v (TL): Hill Street Studios/Blend Images/GettyImages; p. v (BR): Hill Street Studios/Blend Images/GettyImages; p. v (BL): track5/E+/GettyImages; p. v (TR): fstop123/E+/GettyImages; p. 2 (header), p. vi (Unit 1): Tony Anderson/Taxi/GettyImages; p. 2 (T): Steve West/Taxi Japan/GettyImages; p. 2 (B): PhotoInc/E+/GettyImages; p. 4 (CR): Thomas Barwick/Iconica/GettyImages; p. 4 (BR): monkeybusinessimages/GettyImages; p. 5 (T): Shawna Hansen/Moment Open/GettyImages; p. 5 (B): Andersen Ross/Stockbyte/GettyImages; p. 6: Caiaimage/Tom Merton/OJO+/Cultura/GettyImages; p. 7: Heath Korvola/Stone/GettyImages; p. 8 (header), p. vi (Unit 2): Kelvin Murray/Taxi/GettyImages; p. 8 (TR): Paul Bradbury/Caiaimage/GettyImages; p. 8 (Lia): Tetra Images/Brand X Pictures/GettyImages; p. 8 (Josh): NicolasMcComber/E+/GettyImages; p. 8 (Ed): XiXinXing/GettyImages; p. 8 (Rose): Tim Robberts/The Image Bank/GettyImages; p. 8 (Jeff): T2 Images/Cultura/GettyImages; p. 8 (Mei): Yagi Studio/DigitalVision/GettyImages; p. 8 (Anna): Ron Levine/DigitalVision/GettyImages; p. 8 (Mike): Jon Feingersh/Blend Images/GettyImages; p. 9 (student): Nycretoucher/Stone/GettyImages; p. 9 (volunteer): asiseeit/E+/GettyImages; p. 9 (business): Thomas Barwick/Stone/GettyImages; p. 9 (movie set): bjones27/E+/GettyImages; p. 10: Sue Barr/Image Source/GettyImages; p. 11: JP Greenwood/The Image Bank/GettyImages; p. 12: Edge Magazine/Future/Future Publishing/GettyImages; p. 13 (T): Gary Burchell/Taxi/GettyImages; p. 13 (C): Hero Images/GettyImages; p. 13 (B): asiseeit/E+/GettyImages; p. 14: Juanmonino/E+/GettyImages; p. 15 (CR): Hero Images/GettyImages; p. 15 (BR): kali9/E+/GettyImages; p. 16 (header), p. iv (Unit 3): Ascent Xmedia/Stone/GettyImages; p. 16 (T): PeopleImages/DigitalVision/Getty Images Plus/GettyImages; p. 16 (B): Tetra Images/GettyImages; p. 17: Maskot/GettyImages; p. 18 (Sara): Tim Robberts/Taxi/GettyImages; p. 18 (Kim): monkeybusinessimages/iStock/Getty Images Plus/GettyImages; p. 19 (T): Maskot/Maskot/GettyImages; p. 19 (Ex 9): Tetra Images-Rob Lewine/Brand X Pictures/Getty Images; p. 20: Roy Mehta/Iconica/GettyImages; p. 21: Tetra Images/GettyImages; p. 22 (header), p. iv (Unit 4): Tom Merton/Caiaimage/GettyImages; p. 22 (news): Rune Johansen/Photolibrary/GettyImages; p. 22 (health): Peter Dazeley/Photographer's Choice/GettyImages; p. 22 (trending topics): Jess Nichols/EyeEm/GettyImages; p. 22 (arts): Daniel Allan/Cultura/GettyImages; p. 22 (science): Don Klumpp/The Image Bank/GettyImages; p. 22 (tech): Georgijevic/E+/GettyImages; p. 23: Tetra Images/Brand X Pictures/GettyImages; p. 25: Rachel Lewis/Lonely Planet Images/GettyImages; p. 25 (Carol): Jetta Productions/Blend Images/GettyImages; p. 25 (Milo): JohnnyGreig/E+/GettyImages; p. 26: elvira_gumirova/GettyImages; p. 26 (B/G): Anna Bryukhanova/GettyImages; p. 27: artpipi/E+/GettyImages; p. 28: JGI/Jamie Grill/Blend Images/GettyImages; p. 29: Matt Dutile/Image Source/GettyImages; p. 30 (header), p. iv (Unit 5): Image Source/DigitalVision/GettyImages; p. 30 (T): William King/Taxi/GettyImages; p. 30 (B): PBNJ Productions/Blend Images/GettyImages; p. 31: Buena Vista Images/DigitalVision/GettyImages; p. 32: Nachosuch/iStock/Getty Images Plus/GettyImages; p. 33: John Fedele/Blend Images/GettyImages; p. 34 (T): Dave & Les Jacobs/Blend Images/GettyImages; p. 34 (B): Kay Chernush/Stockbyte/GettyImages; p. 35 (B): Westend61/GettyImages; p. 35 (TR): Rafael Elias/Moment/GettyImages; p. 36 (header), p. vi (Unit 6): Caiaimage/Trevor Adeline/Caiaimage/GettyImages; p. 36 (CR): Peter Cade/The Image Bank/GettyImages; p. 37 (photo 1): p6opov/iStock/Getty Images Plus/GettyImages; p. 37 (photo 2): Michael Blann/DigitalVision/GettyImages; p. 37 (photo 3): Shannon Miller/Moment/GettyImages; p. 37 (photo 4): xril/iStock/Getty Images Plus/GettyImages; p. 38 (TR): Creatas/Creatas/Getty Images Plus/GettyImages; p. 38 (BR): Mel Yates/Photodisc/Getty Images Plus/GettyImages; p. 38 (Leory): Monty Rakusen/Cultura/GettyImages; p. 38 (Heather): Sam Edwards/Caiaimage/GettyImages; p. 40: Jupiterimages/PHOTOS.com/Getty Images Plus/GettyImages; p. 41: Image Source/GettyImages; p. 42: Jamie Grill/GettyImages; p. 43: Klaus Vedfelt/DigitalVision/GettyImages; p. 44 (header), p. vi (Unit 7): Hero Images/GettyImages; p. 44 (B): Todd Wright/Blend Images/GettyImages; p. 45 (TL): narvikk/E+/GettyImages; p. 45 (TC): TongRo Images Inc/TongRo Images/GettyImages; p. 45 (TR): Visuals Unlimited, Inc./Thomas Marent/Visuals Unlimited/GettyImages; p. 45 (BL): mshch/iStock/Getty Images Plus/GettyImages; p. 45 (BC): Marcos Alves/Moment/GettyImages; p. 45 (BR): Helmut Meyer zur Capellen/imageBROKER/Getty Images Plus/GettyImages; p. 46: Michael Krasowitz/Photographer's Choice/GettyImages; p. 47: Photofusion/Universal Images Group/GettyImages; p. 48 (TL): jinga80/iStock/Getty Images Plus/GettyImages; p. 48 (TR): sestovic/E+/GettyImages; p. 48 (BL): 101cats/iStock/Getty Images Plus/GettyImages; p. 48 (BR): inFocusDC/iStock/Getty Images Plus/GettyImages; p. 49 (TR): Cigdem Sean Cooper/Moment Open/GettyImages; p. 49 (BL): Antonio Busiello/robertharding/GettyImages; p. 50 (header), p. vi (Unit 8): akindo/DigitalVision Vectors/GettyImages; p. 51: Hill Street Studios/Blend Images/GettyImages; p. 52: Wavebreakmedia Ltd/Wavebreak Media/Getty Images Plus/GettyImages; p. 53: MarioGuti/iStock/Getty Images Plus/GettyImages; p. 54 (T): Dave & Les Jacobs/Blend Images/Getty Images Plus/GettyImages; p. 54 (B): JGI/Jamie Grill/Blend Images/GettyImages; p. 55: Apeloga AB/Cultura/GettyImages; p. 56: John Lund/DigitalVision/GettyImages; p. 57: mediaphotos/iStock/Getty Images Plus/GettyImages; p. 115 (Gaston): Serge Krouglikoff/The Image Bank/GettyImages; p. 115 (Melissa): Sam Edwards/OJO Images/GettyImages; p. 115 (Don): Neustockimages/E+/GettyImages; p. 115 (Emma): Tom Werner/Taxi/GettyImages; p. 115 (Mike): Hero Images/GettyImages; p. 115 (Paola): filadendron/E+/GettyImages; p. 115 (Joanne): digitalskillet/iStock/Getty Images Plus/GettyImages; p. 115 (Ren): Stewart Cohen/Taxi/GettyImages; p. 116 (TL): Bluemoon Stock/Stockbyte/GettyImages; p. 116 (TC): scanrail/iStock/Getty Images Plus/GettyImages; p. 116 (TR): sihuo0860371/iStock/Getty Images Plus/GettyImages; p. 116 (CL): Comstock/Stockbyte/GettyImages; p. 116 (C): EasyBuy4u/E+/GettyImages; p. 116 (CR): Rebekah Logan/Moment Mobile/GettyImages; p. 116 (BL): JosT Elias/Hemera/Getty Images Plus/GettyImages; p. 116 (BC): Zoonar RF/Zoonar/Getty Images Plus/GettyImages; p. 116 (BR): tiler84/iStock/Getty Images Plus/GettyImages; p. 118 (TL): Yellow Dog Productions/The Image Bank/GettyImages; p. 118 (TR): Cultura Exclusive/MoofCultura Exclusive/GettyImages; p. 118 (BL): Alix Minde/PhotoAlto Agency RF Collections/GettyImages; p. 121: Pete Marovich/Getty Images News/Getty Images North America/GettyImages; p. 122: Michael Marquand/Lonely Planet Images/GettyImages.

interchange
FIFTH EDITION

3A

Video Activity Worksheets

Jack C. Richards
Revised by Lynne Robertson

CAMBRIDGE UNIVERSITY PRESS

Credits

Illustration credits

Andrezzinho: 7, 22; Ralph Butler: 17, 40; Paul Daviz: 6, 18 (*top*), 42; Carlos Diaz: 12, 36; Chuck Gonzales: 5, 14 (*top*), 35, 45; Jim Haynes: 2, 34; Trevor Keen: 14 (*bottom*), 44; KJA-artists.com: 4, 54; Robert Schuster: 18 (*bottom*), 56; James Yamasaki: 8, 16, 24

Photography credits

2 ©Fuse/Getty Images; 10 ©Mary Kate Denny/PhotoEdit; 21 ©Monkey Business Images/Shutterstock; 22 ©Steve Dunwell/Ticket/Photolibrary; 25 ©kak2s/Shutterstock; 26 (*top*) ©Peter Harrison/Ticket/Photolibrary; (*bottom*) ©U.S. Coast Guard/Science Faction/SuperStock; 30 (*top*) ©Adalberto Ríos Szalay/Age Fotostock; (*bottom*) ©Comstock Images/Getty Images; 32 (*notebook*) ©Igor A. Bondarenko/Shutterstock; (*clockwise from top left*) ©IMAGEMORE Co., Ltd./Getty Images; ©Nick White/Digital Vision/Getty Images; ©Masterfile; ©Tim Robberts/Riser/Getty Images; 33 ©Erik Isakson/Tetra Images/Corbis; 34 ©forestpath/Shutterstock; 38 (*top row, left to right*) ©06photo/Shutterstock; ©Mixa/Age Fotostock; ©Masterfile; (*bottom row, left to right*) ©David M. Grossman/The Image Works; ©Yuri Arcurs/Shutterstock; 46 ©Lonely Planet/SuperStock; 50 ©Marcia Chambers/dbimages/Alamy; 51 (*center right and right*) ©Adam Stanford/Aerial-Cam Photography; 52 (*left to right*) ©Scherl/SZ Photo/The Image Works; ©Nataiki/Shutterstock; 54 ©Collage Photography/Veer; 58 ©Spencer Platt/Getty Images; 60 ©Brigette Sullivan/PhotoEdit; ©David Grossman/Alamy

Video credits

Unit 7 ©BBC Worldwide Americas Inc. Used with permission. Unit 10 ©ABC News. Used with permission. Footage from The Crayon Marketing Firm used with permission.

Unit 13 ©A&E Television Networks. All rights reserved. Used with permission. Unit 16 courtesy of *60 Minutes*. ©Copyright CBS News. Used with permission.

Plan of Video 3A

1 Dream Date p. 2 A young woman chooses one of three men for her date on a dating game show.
Functional Focus Expressing feelings; describing personalities
Grammar Clauses containing *it* with adverbial clauses
Vocabulary Adjectives to describe personalities

2 Career moves p. 6 A career advisor talks about the importance of someone's personality type in choosing a major and profession.
Functional Focus Describing personality types
Grammar Gerunds as subjects and objects
Vocabulary Words related to jobs and personality types

3 Common ground p. 10 A woman asks her friend to look after her younger sister overnight.
Functional Focus Asking favors
Grammar Indirect requests
Vocabulary Requests and responses

4 Around the campfire p. 14 Three friends on a camping trip share a spooky story and meet a mysterious stranger.
Functional Focus Telling a story in the past
Grammar Past tense verbs: past continuous, simple past, past perfect
Vocabulary Unusual events

5 Travel World p. 18 Reporters around the world ask people about cross-cultural experiences.
Functional Focus Describing customs
Grammar Expectations: (*not*) *expected to*, (*not*) *supposed to*, (*not*) *customary to*, (*not*) *acceptable to*
Vocabulary Words related to traveling abroad

6 What's the problem? p. 22 A couple's hope for a relaxing weekend at a quaint hotel is dashed.
Functional Focus Describing problems; making complaints
Grammar *Need* with passive infinitives and gerunds
Vocabulary Words to describe problems

7 Endangered islands p. 26 A BBC reporter explains how climate change threatens the island nation of Tuvalu.
Functional Focus Describing environmental problems
Grammar The passive and prepositions of cause
Vocabulary Words related to the environment and climate change

8 Tango! p. 30 A reporter talks to several people about learning to dance the tango.
Functional Focus Talking about learning methods
Grammar Gerunds and infinitives; *would rather* and *would prefer*
Vocabulary Words related to learning

1 Dream Date

Preview

1 CULTURE

In North America, many people start dating in their teens and early twenties. They meet at school or work, or they're introduced by friends. On dates, they go out in couples or in groups to movies, sporting events, and meals. Traditionally, the man paid for the date, but modern couples may decide to split the bill or let the person who made the invitation pay for both people.

How do people in your country meet each other? What do friends or dating couples like to do together? Where are some popular places to go? When a man and a woman (or a group of friends) go out together, who pays?

2 VOCABULARY Personality types

PAIR WORK How would you describe the people below? Choose a description from the box.

a good conversationalist	easygoing	generous
ambitious	✓ egotistical	straightforward

1. Jill is always talking about herself. She thinks she's better than other people.
   A: I think she's *egotistical*.
   B: Yes, I agree.
2. Mike is very relaxed. Nothing seems to upset him.
3. Paul always tells people exactly what he thinks. He doesn't hide his feelings.
4. Erika has big plans and works hard to achieve them.
5. John asks a lot of questions, and he's interested in what I have to say.
6. Leah is a great friend. She gives others a lot of her time and energy, and she also forgives others easily.

3 GUESS THE STORY

Elizabeth is going to choose one of these men to be her date. How do you think she will decide? Who will she choose?

Bachelor 1   Bachelor 2   Bachelor 3

Watch the video

4 GET THE PICTURE

A Look at your answers to Exercise 3. Did you guess correctly?

B Check (✓) the things Elizabeth said to the bachelors. Then compare with a partner.

☐ Describe to me your ideal date.
☐ How old are you?
☐ What's your favorite sport?
☐ Tell me two things about yourself: one positive and one negative.
☐ Finish this sentence: "I think it's disgusting when . . ."
☐ Finish this sentence: "My ideal date has . . ."

C What words describe Elizabeth and the bachelors? Write the correct word under each picture. Then compare with a partner.

| easygoing | egotistical | excited | straightforward |

[1] [2] [3] [4]

5 WATCH FOR DETAILS

Correct the mistakes below. Then compare with a partner.

Bachelor 1 is a ~~reporter~~ *writer* and a former college soccer coach who loves playing or watching almost every kind of game. Bachelor 2 is a model, who also studies languages. Everyone should recognize him from his latest jeans ad on buses and in magazines. Bachelor 3 is the Director of Educational Programs at a high school. In his free time, he enjoys swimming, running, and dancing. He and Elizabeth went to college together.

Interchange VRB 3 © Cambridge University Press 2012   Photocopiable   Unit 1 ▪ 3

6 WHO SAID WHAT?

Who said the sentences below? Check (✓) the correct answers. Then compare with a partner.

	Bachelor 1	Bachelor 2	Bachelor 3
1. I'd be too embarrassed to tell you the truth.	☐	☐	☐
2. It bothers me when people lie.	☐	☐	☐
3. It's hard to split my time among so many people!	☐	☐	☐
4. I'd take you out for a nice dinner.	☐	☐	☐
5. I think I'm a pretty good friend, very reliable.	☐	☐	☐
6. Well, I'm actually a pretty good guy.	☐	☐	☐
7. I'd probably say I had car trouble.	☐	☐	☐

Follow-up

7 ROLE PLAY Let's play Dream Date!

A PAIR WORK Imagine you are Elizabeth. Add two more questions to ask the bachelors.

1. Describe to me your ideal date.
2. Tell me two things about yourself: one positive and one negative.
3. Finish this sentence: "I can't stand it when . . . "
4. ....
5. ....

B GROUP WORK Now join another pair. Three of you are bachelors. The fourth person is Elizabeth.

Elizabeth: Take turns asking the three bachelors your questions. Then choose your dream date.

Bachelors: Answer Elizabeth's questions. Try to get Elizabeth to choose you as her dream date.

Language close-up

8 WHAT DID THEY SAY?

Watch the video and complete the conversation. Then practice it.

Elizabeth is asking the bachelors to complete a few sentences.

Elizabeth: Bachelor Number 1, finish this sentence:
"I ……………… ……………… it when …"

Bachelor 1: I ……………… ……………… it when … people ……………… when I'm ……………… ……………… ……………… the soccer match on TV.

Elizabeth: Bachelor Number 3, finish this sentence:
"I ……………… it's ……………… when …"

Bachelor 3: I ……………… it's ……………… when … when I go to a fancy ……………… and I don't get the ……………… I deserve.

Elizabeth: Bachelor Number 2, finish this sentence: "It ……………… ……………… me when …"

Bachelor 2: It ……………… ……………… me when … people ……………… over unimportant things. I just think people should be less ……………… and more ……………… .

9 CLAUSES CONTAINING IT WITH ADVERBIAL CLAUSES

A Complete the sentences about dates or friendships with phrases from the box. Then add two more statements of your own.

> ✓ arrive late
> forget to call me
> lie to me
> make me feel special
> send me flowers
> talk during a movie

1. I can't stand it *when my date arrives late* .
2. It makes me happy ……………… .
3. I like it ……………… .
4. It bothers me ……………… .
5. It really upsets me ……………… .
6. It embarrasses me ……………… .
7. ……………… .
8. ……………… .

B **PAIR WORK** Compare your statements with a partner. Which of your partner's statements are true for you?

2 Career moves

Preview

1 CULTURE

Choosing a career can be difficult if you're not sure what job is best for you. Experts suggest the following to help you make a decision:
- Take a career assessment test to find out what professions are a good match for you.
- Look at your educational and work achievements to determine your strengths and weaknesses.
- Think about your hobbies and free-time activities, and what they say about your interests, abilities, and values.
- Talk with a friend or family member who is a good listener, or consult with a career counselor.

Talk about your career plans. Which skills and abilities would you use in this future career? How is this type of work related to what you want to accomplish in life? How sure are you of your current career choice?

2 VOCABULARY Attributes at work

A Complete each sentence with a word from the box.

| creative | collaborative | ✓ independent | physical | practical | precise |

1. My brother is very ...independent..., so he prefers to work by himself.
2. My friend Elena is a graphic designer, which lets her use her imagination and be _____ .
3. My boss comes up with the big ideas, but I enjoy planning out the _____ details.
4. Building a house requires _____ strength and stamina.
5. The best part of working in a team is the _____ process of making decisions together.
6. In finance, it's important to be _____ and not make mistakes!

B PAIR WORK Describe yourself or someone you know well. Your partner describes the person's personality using one of the words from the box.

A: My friend makes a list of all the things he has to do each day.
B: He sounds like a practical person.

6 • Unit 2

3 GUESS THE STORY

Watch the first minute of the video with the sound off.
Answer these questions.

1. Where is the conversation taking place?
2. Who do you think the man and woman are?
3. What do you think they are discussing?

Watch the video

4 GET THE PICTURE

A Look at your answers to Exercise 3. Did you guess correctly?

B What personality type did Ms. Auden think would be best suited to the jobs below? Write the correct word under each picture. Then compare with a partner.

1	2	3	4
librarian	repair person	teacher	lawyer

5 MAKING INFERENCES

Which statements are probably true? Which are probably false?
Check (✓) your answers. Then compare with a partner.

	True	False
1. A conventional type would make a good actor.	☐	☐
2. Good waiters are often social types.	☐	☐
3. An enterprising type would not work for other people.	☐	☐
4. Most accountants are artistic types.	☐	☐
5. Someone who runs his or her own business is an investigative type.	☐	☐
6. Mechanics are often realistic types.	☐	☐
7. Studying animals in the wild would appeal to some investigative types.	☐	☐

6 WHAT'S YOUR OPINION?

A Read the description of each person's personality type below. Then write notes in the chart about which job at an advertising agency you think the person would enjoy, if any. Be sure to give reasons.

	Manager	Ad designer	Accountant
1. Bernie is a conventional type.	No; prefers to follow rules and procedures	No; doesn't enjoy creative things as much	Yes; likes details
2. Fatima is an enterprising type.			
3. Yoko is an investigative type.			
4. Carlos is an artistic type.			

B GROUP WORK Compare your answers with your group. Come up with one other job at the agency that would suit each person.

Follow-up

7 ARE THEY DOING THE RIGHT JOBS?

A Write the names of three people you know well. Tell what job each one does. Then describe each worker's personality type and explain why his or her job is right for them.

Name	Job	Personality type
My brother	Manager of a men's clothing store	Conventional; good for him because he likes people and he's organized
1.		
2.		
3.		

B PAIR WORK Take turns describing each person you wrote about to your partner. Answer any questions your partner may have.

8 ▪ Unit 2

Language close-up

8 WHAT DID THEY SAY?

Watch the video and complete the conversation. Then practice it.

Jacquelyn Auden talks with Jamie about personality types.

Ms. Auden: There are six .... personality types: ...., conventional, enterprising, investigative, realistic, and .... The .... type is artistic. These .... are .... and imaginative, and they .... to work on one .... at a time, rather than multi-tasking.

Jamie: What .... should artistic .... pursue?

Ms. Auden: The most .... thing for .... type of people is being in .... of a .... project. So, ... to consider are landscaping, graphic ...., web design.

Jamie: I .... The .... personality type is conventional. Tell us .... that one.

Ms. Auden: Yes. Conventional types are .... and orderly. They .... well to rules, ..., schedules, ... like that.

9 GERUNDS AS SUBJECTS AND OBJECTS *Describing a job*

A Complete the sentences about a job using the gerund forms of the words and phrases in the box. Then guess the job described.

| encourage | organize the game schedule | work on weekends |
| improve their skills | stay in shape | ✓ work with children |

1. I enjoy ....working with children.... ; it helps me feel young.
2. .... is easy with all the running around I have to do.
3. I don't always enjoy ...., but that's when our games are held.
4. At the end of the season, we have a big tournament, so I spend a lot of time .... for that event.
5. I help players concentrate on ....
6. .... weaker players helps the whole team improve.

Job described: ....

B PAIR WORK Choose a job and describe your duties. Can your partner guess your job?

Interchange VRB 3 © Cambridge University Press 2012   Photocopiable   Unit 2 ▪ 9

3 Common ground

Preview

1 CULTURE

Read this advice to babysitters in North America.
- Ask parents to show you the location of emergency exits, smoke detectors, and fire extinguishers.
- Make sure you have the telephone number of where the parents are going.
- If the children are up, know their location at all times and never leave them alone for too long. If the children are asleep, check on them about every fifteen minutes.
- Always get approval if you would like to have a visitor.
- In an emergency, call 911. Identify yourself by name, say you are babysitting, and state the problem. Say where you are and give the phone number you are calling from.

Is babysitting popular in your country? What would you enjoy about babysitting? What would be challenging? Write some suggestions or rules for babysitters to add to the list above.

2 VOCABULARY Requests and responses

PAIR WORK Match each request with a response. Then practice the requests and responses.

_d_ 1. Is it all right if I use your phone?
____ 2. Would you mind my using your car?
____ 3. Is it OK if I drop her off?
____ 4. Could you ask her to bring something?
____ 5. I was wondering if you could help me out.
____ 6. Would you mind if she stayed with you?

a. No, go ahead. The keys are on the table.
b. OK. I'll tell her.
c. Sure. What can I do?
d. No, sorry. I'm expecting a call.
e. Not at all. I'd be happy to have her.
f. Sure. Or I can pick her up.

3 GUESS THE STORY

Watch the first minute of the video with the sound off.
What do you think the women are talking about?

Watch the video

4 GET THE PICTURE

First put the pictures in order (1 to 6). Then write the correct request under each picture. Compare with a partner.

Could you please turn down the volume?
Is it OK if I watch the movie now?
Could I have something to eat?
Can we watch them?
Would you mind if she stayed with you tonight?
Could we watch the second movie after this one is over?

5 MAKING INFERENCES

Which statements are probably true? Which are probably false? Check (✓) your answers. Then compare with a partner.

	True	False
1. Anne is in a hurry.	☐	☐
2. Anne and Megan live together.	☐	☐
3. Rachel thinks it will be easy to get along with Megan.	☐	☐
4. Rachel is worried that Megan might interfere with her work.	☐	☐
5. Megan doesn't want to do her homework.	☐	☐
6. Megan doesn't care what food she eats.	☐	☐
7. Anne is surprised that Megan and Rachel became friends.	☐	☐

6 WHO SAID WHAT?

Who said the sentences below? Check (✓) the correct answers. Then compare with a partner.

	Anne	Rachel	Megan
1. I need a big favor.	☐	☐	☐
2. Hey, you've got the *Twilight* movies!	☐	☐	☐
3. How's the homework coming?	☐	☐	☐
4. I'm starving.	☐	☐	☐
5. You've never read any of the books or seen the movies?	☐	☐	☐
6. You two really seemed to hit it off.	☐	☐	☐

Follow-up

7 ROLE PLAY

A PAIR WORK

Student A: You're planning a big party for this weekend. You want your friend (Student B) to help you. Write your requests in the box below. Then ask your friend for help.

Student B: Accept or decline your friend's (Student A's) requests.

1. I was wondering if I could borrow your vacuum cleaner.
2. ....
3. ....

A: I was wondering if I could borrow your vacuum cleaner.
B: Of course. Go right ahead!

B PAIR WORK

Student B: You're moving to a new apartment. You want your friend (Student A) to help you. Write your requests in the box below. Then ask your friend for help.

Student A: Accept or decline your friend's (Student B's) requests.

1. Is it OK if I borrow these boxes?
2. ....
3. ....

Language close-up

8 WHAT DID THEY SAY?

Watch the video and complete the conversation. Then practice it.

Anne asks her friend Rachel for a favor.

Anne: Rachel! I am so _____ you're home. I was _____ if you could help me out.

Rachel: Yeah. _____ _____, Anne?

Anne: I _____ a big _____. My _____ just called, and he wants me to go out of town _____ _____ to meet with a client.

Rachel: _____ _____.

Anne: Yeah. But my _____ are out of town, too, and my little sister, Megan, is _____ with me. _____ _____ if she stayed with you _____? I _____ pick her up _____ by ten.

Rachel: No, I _____ _____ at all. What _____ did you want to _____ her over?

Anne: How about _____?

9 INDIRECT REQUESTS *Asking favors*

A Anne has asked Rachel to look after her apartment while she is away. Anne has several requests for Rachel. Complete their phone conversation with the correct form of the expressions in the box.

Anne: Would you mind *taking in the mail every day*?
Rachel: Sure, no problem. I'll leave it on the table.
Anne: Great. And could you _____?
Rachel: I'd love to. I've got some fish at home.
Anne: And let's see. I was wondering if you could _____?
Rachel: Sure. I'll water them once a day.
Anne: Great. Oh, and I was wondering if you'd mind _____?
Rachel: Yeah, I guess. How often does he need a walk?
Anne: Only three times a day. Anyway, one more thing. Is it OK if Megan _____?
Rachel: Are you kidding? Of course it's OK. Megan and I get along just fine.

feed the fish
spend the weekend
✓take in the mail every day
water the plants
walk the dog

B **PAIR WORK** Imagine you are going away for a weekend, and your partner is going to look after your apartment or house. Write several requests. Then take turns asking each other the favors.

4 Around the campfire

Preview

1 CULTURE

North Americans enjoy telling stories, especially spooky stories about scary and mysterious things. Spooky stories are popular around the campfire, at sleepovers, and during the fall and winter months, especially near Halloween. People tell and listen to these stories as a way of dealing with their fear of the unknown. It's also fun to experience the thrill of fear while knowing that you're really safe.

Do you enjoy telling and listening to stories? Do you enjoy spooky or scary stories? Why or why not? Are stories about mysterious people and events popular in your culture? If you can, share a well-known story from your culture with some classmates.

2 VOCABULARY Descriptions

For each pair of pictures write the correct description.

1. surprised / freaked out

   freaked out
   surprised

2. .... / ....

   a mysterious situation
   a scary situation

3. .... / ....

   a scream
   a hoot

4. .... / ....

   a farm
   a campground

14 ▪ Unit 4

3 GUESS THE STORY

Check (✓) what you think is happening in each of the following situations.

☐ She has just taken a shower.
☐ She has just gone on a hike.

☐ She is going to make dinner.
☐ She is going to tell a story.

☐ He is greeting the girls.
☐ He is telling a spooky story.

VIDEO ACTIVITIES

Watch the video

4 GET THE PICTURE

A Check your answers to Exercise 3. Did you guess correctly?

B Check (✓) **True** or **False**. Correct the false statements. Then compare with a partner.

	True	False	
1. Ellen heard a story at the restaurant.	☐	☐	....
2. Molly doesn't like scary stories.	☐	☐	....
3. The campground used to be a farm.	☐	☐	....
4. Ted McShane died in a fire.	☐	☐	....

5 WATCH FOR DETAILS

Complete the sentences. Then compare your answers with a partner.

1. Ellen overheard a woman telling this story to her ......daughter...... .
2. Vanessa tells Molly not to be a ....
3. The McShanes inherited the farm from a ....
4. When the McShanes walked down the street, they always ....
5. Every evening, Mr. McShane brought his wife ....
6. Mr. McShane's wife was named ....
7. The girls get frightened when .... arrives.

Interchange VRB 3 © Cambridge University Press 2012   Photocopiable   *Unit 4* ■ 15

6 MAKING INFERENCES

Which statements are probably true? Which are probably false? Check (✓) your answers. Then compare with a partner.

	True	False
1. Vanessa likes scary stories.	☐	☐
2. The man in the story was a farmer.	☐	☐
3. The fire started because of a hot and dry summer.	☐	☐
4. The park ranger wanted to scare the girls.	☐	☐
5. Vanessa is embarrassed that they were so easily frightened.	☐	☐
6. The ranger is the same person from the story.	☐	☐

Follow-up

7 DO YOU BELIEVE THESE STORIES?

GROUP WORK Read the descriptions of the creatures below. Do you believe they ever existed? Do you think they exist now? Have conversations like this:

A: Do you think the Loch Ness Monster exists?
B: I think it's just a story. There are no such things as monsters!
C: I hate to disagree, but many people say that they have seen strange creatures.

The Loch Ness Monster, Scotland

This creature was first seen in 565 BCE, and sightings are still reported every year. Some people believe that it is a dinosaur, an eel, or a type of whale. Many photos of "Nessie" have been taken, but some have turned out to be fakes and others are too dark or blurry to really show the creature.

Alien Big Cats, England

Some people believe that large, wild cats, such as panthers and leopards, exist in some areas of the English countryside. Called "alien" because they are foreign (not extraterrestrial!), none has ever been captured. Photos and videos have never been clear enough to prove their existence, yet there have been as many as 2,000 sightings in a single year.

Language close-up

8 WHAT DID THEY SAY?

Watch the video and complete the conversation. Then practice it.

The ranger surprises the girls while Ellen is telling the story.

Ranger: Oh, I'm .... I didn't mean to .... you ladies. I was making my .... and .... to see if .... is all right.

Molly: Yes. A park ranger, of .... Yes, everything's .... Ellen was .... us a .... story when you came by.

Ranger: Campfire ...., huh? That's .... fun. Well, OK, then. I'll let you .... back to it.

Vanessa: Thanks for .... on us. And sorry .... the ....

Ranger: That's OK. I'm .... to it. Hey, in the .... you .... should take a look .... that path. There's a .... full of wildflowers, and .... in bloom right now – very ....

Vanessa: Oh! That's good to .... We'll .... that. Thanks.

9 PAST TENSE VERBS Telling a story

A Write the correct form of the verbs in parentheses (past perfect, past continuous, or simple past) to complete this story.

Last Saturday, I .... (walk) down Elm Street when I .... (notice) something strange. A very fancy sports car .... (sit) in front of the entrance to the First Bank building. No one .... (be) in the car, but the engine .... (run). I .... (stop) next to the car to take a look. It was the first time I .... (see) a car like that. Suddenly, a man with a large bag .... (run) out of the bank and .... (jump) into the car. He .... (drive) away so fast, he almost .... (hit) me. Then I realized: I .... (witness) a bank robbery!

B PAIR WORK

A: Think of something unusual that has happened to you. Tell a story about what happened.
B: Listen and ask questions. Then change roles.

Interchange VRB 3 © Cambridge University Press 2012   Photocopiable

5 Travel World

Preview

1 CULTURE

Culture shock, the emotional and physical distress you may feel when you visit a foreign country or culture, has three stages. The first stage, sometimes called the "honeymoon" stage, is characterized by exaggerated happiness and excitement. In the second stage, you might feel angry or sad at not being able to communicate or understand the other culture. You might even get physically ill. Finally, in the third stage, you realize that the new culture offers rewards as well as challenges, and you feel ready and able to adapt to a new lifestyle.

Have you ever seen a visitor to your country experiencing culture shock? What kind of person do you think experiences culture shock the most severely? the least severely? Have you ever experienced culture shock? Describe your experiences.

2 VOCABULARY Travel abroad

Put the words below in the word map. Add at least one more word to each list. Then compare answers with a partner.

afraid to make a mistake	eating a huge meal at lunch	shaking hands
beautiful	kissing in public	spectacular
confused	picturesque	surprised

Customs

Feelings
afraid to make a mistake

Scenery

18 ▪ Unit 5

3 GUESS THE FACTS

What things do you think cause people to experience culture shock?

- ☐ climate
- ☐ clothing
- ☐ families
- ☐ food
- ☐ greetings
- ☐ hotels
- ☐ language
- ☐ transportation

Watch the video

4 GET THE PICTURE

A Check your answers from Exercise 3. Then compare with a partner.

B Complete the information for each person.

Camilla
Lives in: ....
Visited: ....

Andrew
Is from: ....
Lives in: ....

Delfino
Is from: ....
Lives in: ....

5 GUESSING MEANING FROM CONTEXT

Read these sentences from the video. Guess the meanings of the underlined words. Check (✓) your answers. Then compare with a partner.

1. When you get home, you often have some interesting and perhaps humorous stories to tell about your cross-cultural experiences.
   - ☐ experiences that made you angry
   - ✓ experiences in different cultures
   - ☐ experiences in similar cultures

2. Rio de Janeiro – that picturesque city of beautiful beaches, Carnaval, and the samba.
   - ☐ old-fashioned
   - ☐ expensive
   - ☐ pretty

3. You're invading my space.
   - ☐ making me uncomfortable
   - ☐ taking too much of my time
   - ☐ causing me pain

4. It is customary in my culture to have a huge meal in the middle of the day.
   - ☐ rare
   - ☐ polite
   - ☐ usual

Interchange VRB 3 © Cambridge University Press 2012   Photocopiable

Unit 5 ■ 19

6 WATCH FOR DETAILS

According to the video, to which country do the following customs refer? Write the name of a country next to each custom.

Brazil   Sweden
Mexico   the United States
Peru

1. People shake hands when they meet.   ....
2. It's customary to eat a huge meal around noon.   ....
3. People kiss on the cheek when they meet.   ....
4. People often eat just a soup and sandwich for lunch.   ....
5. Bus drivers call out to people on the street.   ....

7 WHAT'S YOUR OPINION?

A Which customs and situations discussed in the video would make you feel uncomfortable when visiting a foreign country? Rank them from 1 (most uncomfortable) to 6 (least uncomfortable).

.... using public transportation   .... having only soup and a sandwich for lunch

.... greeting someone by kissing on the cheeks .... using a private bus system

.... eating a huge meal in the middle of the day .... greeting someone by shaking hands

B **PAIR WORK** Take turns talking about the customs. Use sentences like these:

One thing I'd be most uncomfortable about . . .   The thing that I'd be most uncomfortable about . . .
Something I wouldn't be uncomfortable about . . .   The thing that I'd be least uncomfortable about . . .

Follow-up

8 CROSSING CULTURES

A Choose a country you know well. Make a list of customs that visitors to that country might find different or unusual. Complete the chart.

Country	Customs	
....	....	....
	....	....

B **PAIR WORK** Take turns asking about the customs in the countries you and your partner chose in part A.

20 • Unit 5

Language close-up

9 WHAT DID HE SAY?

Watch the video to complete the commentary. Then compare with a partner.

Chris Brooks talks about culture shock.

Hi. I'm Chris Brooks. .... to *Travel World*. Have you ever .... to a .... with a .... different .... ? If you have, you .... know what "....................." is. It's a feeling of .... you get from .... being in a new .... The .... and .... may seem .... are different. You don't know exactly what you're .... do. You may .... be a little .... of making a .... In ...., you get .... everything. But .... you get ...., you often have some .... and perhaps .... stories to .... about your .... experiences.

10 EXPECTATIONS *Noun, adjective, and verb forms*

A Complete the sentences about expectations with the correct word in parentheses.

1. It is .... (tradition / traditional) to have a large meal at noon in Mexico.
2. You are .... (expected / expectation) to kiss people on both cheeks in Brazil.
3. It is .... (custom / customary) for people to take public transportation in Peru.
4. Are you .... (suppose / supposed) to kiss people on both cheeks in Mexico?
5. My family has a .... (tradition / traditional) of eating dessert at every meal.
6. What is the .... (custom / customary) of greeting people in your country?
7. I didn't have any .... (expect / expectations) about what life was like in Peru.
8. What do you .... (suppose / supposed) I should do when I want more food?

B **PAIR WORK** Compare your statements with a partner.

6 What's the problem?

Preview

1 CULTURE

Travelers in North America looking for quaint, old-fashioned charm or personalized service sometimes choose to stay in a bed and breakfast, or "B & B." Herb and Ruth Boven opened Castle in the Country in Allegan, Michigan. "Our guests come here to relax, enjoy the countryside, or shop at antique markets and specialty shops," says Ruth. Castle in the Country offers special mystery or romance weekends and services such as horse-drawn wagon rides and holiday dinners. "We enjoy meeting guests from different states and countries and showing them what's special about our area."

Have you ever stayed in a B & B? Would you like to stay in one? Talk about different types of hotels in your country with your classmates.

2 VOCABULARY Problems

Complete the sentences with words from the box. Then match each sentence with a picture. Compare with a partner.

cracked	scratched
✓ dirty	stained
broken	stuck
peeling	fixed

1. The room needs cleaning. It's very ……… dirty ……… .
2. The paint is coming off the walls. It's ……………………… .
3. Oh, no. I spilled jam on my shirt. Now it's ……………………… .
4. My cat sharpened her claws on the table. Now it's ……………………… .
5. I dropped the glass on the floor and now it's ……………………… .
6. I can't open the window. It's ……………………… .
7. The remote control works now. It's ……………………… .
8. The cup isn't completely broken, but it is ……………………… .

22 ▪ Unit 6

3 GUESS THE STORY

Check (✓) what you think is happening in each of the following situations.

☐ The older man is checking in.
☐ The older man is giving instructions.

☐ The couple is here to relax.
☐ The couple is here on business.

☐ The man is calling home.
☐ The man is calling the front desk.

Watch the video

4 GET THE PICTURE

Complete the chart. Check (✓) the word that describes each problem. More than one answer may be possible.

	broken	dirty	peeling	scratched	stuck
1. temperature control	☐	☐	☐	☐	☐
2. paint	☐	☐	☐	☐	☐
3. furniture	☐	☐	☐	☐	☐
4. window	☐	☐	☐	☐	☐
5. rug	☐	☐	☐	☐	☐

5 WATCH FOR DETAILS

Complete the sentences with **George**, **Norman**, **Ed**, or **Michelle**.

1. .... needs to go to the hardware store.
2. .... says they don't have much luggage.
3. .... thinks the front desk clerk is strange.
4. .... checks the couple into the hotel.
5. .... calls the front desk to report a problem.
6. .... tries to repair the window.
7. .... says it feels cold in the room.
8. .... returns after the guests leave.

VIDEO ACTIVITIES

Unit 6 ■ 23

6 WHAT'S YOUR OPINION?

PAIR WORK Answer these questions.

1. Do you agree with Michelle and Ed's decision to check out of the hotel? What would you have done?
2. Think of an experience you've had where there were problems. What were the problems? What did you do to solve them?

Follow-up

7 ROLE PLAY

A PAIR WORK How many problems can you find in the picture below? Take turns describing the problems to each other.

B GROUP WORK Now join another pair. Three of you are customers. The fourth person is the waiter.

   Customers: Complain to the waiter about the problems in the restaurant.

   Waiter: Offer solutions to the customers' complaints.

Start like this:

Customer 1: Excuse me, but our dinners are cold.

   Waiter: Oh, I'm sorry. I'll take them back and heat them up.

Customer 2: OK. That would be fine.

Customer 3: Actually, could I order something else instead?

Language close-up

8 WHAT DID THEY SAY?

Watch the video and complete the conversation. Then practice it.

Ed and Michelle complain to Norman about their room.

Norman: Hi. What's the .... ?
Michelle: Oh, it's ....
Norman: .... the heat.
Ed: The heat ....
Norman: Well, what's .... with it?
Michelle: The dial's .... It came off in my ....
Norman: That should .... it.
Ed: .... That window needs .... , too.
It's .... and it's letting the .... air in.
Norman: That should .... it.
Michelle: .... ?
Norman: You're ....

9 NEED WITH PASSIVE INFINITIVES AND GERUNDS

A Read the list of additional problems at the hotel that Norman needs to fix. Then write two sentences with *need* for each problem. Use the verbs in the box.

Norman's List
- [ ] the heat is stuck on high
- [ ] the wastebasket is full
- [ ] the chair is damaged
- [ ] the hair dryer is broken
- [ ] the rooms are dirty
- [ ] the floors are dirty

✓ adjust   fix
clean   repair
empty   wash

1. The heat needs adjusting. / The heat needs to be adjusted.
2. ....
3. ....
4. ....
5. ....
6. ....

B Now think of two things that need to be done at your school or at your home. Then write two sentences to describe what needs to be done.

1. ....
2. ....

Unit 6 ▪ 25

7 Endangered islands

Preview

1 CULTURE

Scientists estimate that the average temperature on Earth has increased by about 0.6 degrees Celsius (one degree Fahrenheit) in the last century. They call this phenomenon global warming, or climate change. Sea levels have risen dramatically because of global warming, increasing as much as eight inches in some places. Low-lying areas and islands are in danger of being covered by the rising water. Some experts predict that if the rising tides continue, many islands and coastal areas around the world will become uninhabitable.

What do you know about the causes of global warming? What effect do you think rising sea levels might have on your country? What other effects do you think global warming might have?

2 VOCABULARY Environmental change

Complete the sentences with phrases from the box. Compare with a partner.

| catastrophic event | coastal areas | global warming |
| climate panel | high tide | technological fix |

1. Less than two days after the levees broke in New Orleans during Hurricane Katrina, 80 percent of the city was under water. It was a ….catastrophic event…. .
2. Engineers are likely to search for a ……………………… to a problem, rather than a natural solution or a change in how people behave.
3. Tsunamis are usually more damaging to the ……………………… of a country than the inland areas.
4. The government appointed a ……………………… made up of scientific experts to find out how changing weather patterns might affect the country in the future.
5. Many scientists believe that ……………………… is causing the glaciers to melt.
6. During a ………………………, many areas by the ocean that are usually above ground may be under water.

26 ▪ Unit 7

3 GUESS THE FACTS

Watch the first two minutes of the video with the sound off. Which of the following do you think are concerns of people living on the island of Tuvalu?

- ☐ cold water
- ☐ high tides
- ☐ unsafe drinking water
- ☐ flooding
- ☐ hot weather
- ☐ strong winds

Watch the video

4 GET THE PICTURE

A Look at your answers to Exercise 3. Did you guess correctly? Correct your answers. Then compare with a partner.

B What are some threats faced by the people living on Tuvalu? Match each threat with the correct picture.

1. Forecasts show that the tides will continue to get higher.
2. The main roads on the island are sometimes flooded.
3. The airport runway may disappear.
4. Plants won't grow in the salty water.

5 WATCH FOR DETAILS

Fill in the blanks. Then compare with a partner.

1. It's difficult to grow anything on Tuvalu because the soil is too ....
2. An Australian system has been monitoring the tides in Tuvalu for .... years.
3. Scientists predict that most coastal areas of Tuvalu will be washed out in .... years.
4. A typical high tide reaches about .... meters.
5. The highest point on Tuvalu is only about .... meters.
6. Without help, Tuvalu can survive for only about .... more years.
7. The island nation of Tuvalu has .... inhabitants.

6 GUESSING MEANING FROM CONTEXT

Read these sentences from the video. Choose the best meaning of each underlined word. Check (✓) your answers. Then compare with a partner.

1. Incredibly beautiful, but incredibly vulnerable.
   ☐ expensive ☐ easily damaged ☐ ancient

2. The water also surges up from underground, through the coral the islands are built on.
   ☐ floats ☐ moves sideways ☐ rises suddenly

3. This isn't like other floods that I've covered, with a single catastrophic event.
   ☐ fortunate ☐ terrible ☐ interesting

4. At the harbor, the rising swell is monitored by an Australian system.
   ☐ controlled ☐ ignored ☐ measured

5. These [islands] are so narrow, you can cross from one side to the other in a few short paces.
   ☐ steps ☐ miles ☐ minutes

Follow-up

7 FOR OR AGAINST

A PAIR WORK Imagine you are in charge of an organization that is considering helping the island nation of Tuvalu. List three reasons for and against trying to save these islands.

For	Against
....	....
....	....
....	....

B GROUP WORK Now join another pair. Discuss the reasons you listed. Use language like this:

In my opinion . . .
That's an interesting idea. However, . . .
I feel that . . .

On the other hand . . .
That's a good point. Nevertheless, . . .
I don't think that . . .

Language close-up

8 WHAT DID HE SAY?

Watch the video and complete the commentary. Then compare with a partner.

A reporter is talking about what Tuvalu needs to survive.

For the children of Tuvalu, the .... are fun. But for them to .... their .... on these islands will require .... international .... And with .... 11,000 people here, will the .... world think it's .... it? Now, of course, Tuvalu does get some .... , but not .... enough to keep the .... sea at bay. So the .... community .... very soon a difficult .... of .... to draw a line between .... who get .... and those who don't. And in the .... , people here are getting ready for .... king tide. Right now it's .... ; it's due to get very .... in about eight hours' time.

9 THE PASSIVE

Rewrite these sentences from the active to the passive. Use the prepositions in parentheses to indicate the cause. Then compare with a partner.

1. King tides are washing out some of Tuvalu's coastal areas. (because of)
   Some of Tuvalu's coastal areas are being washed out because of king tides.

2. Salty seawater is killing off most of the plant life. (due to)
   ....
   ....

3. An Australian system monitors the changes in sea level on Tuvalu. (by)
   ....
   ....

4. In five to ten years, rising sea levels will cover many coastal areas. (as a result of)
   ....
   ....

5. The international community must set up a global fund to save Tuvalu. (by)
   ....
   ....

Interchange VRB 3 © Cambridge University Press 2012   Photocopiable

8 Tango!

Preview

1 CULTURE

Tango dancing began in Argentina and Uruguay in the mid-1800s. The music of tango blended African, Cuban, and European elements. Over time, tango music and tango dancing united people from many different cultures and social classes in South America. As sailors from Argentina traveled to Europe and North America, they taught the dance to local residents, and its popularity spread. Today there are tango schools all over the world, and new styles of the dance are constantly evolving. One of the latest styles, *nuevo tango*, brings in electronic and alternative music and adds new life to this ever-popular dance form.

Why do you think people like to dance? Give as many reasons as you can. What kinds of dances are popular in your country? What kinds have you tried? What kinds of music are popular in your country now? Are there dances that go with each type of music?

2 VOCABULARY Learning

A **PAIR WORK** What are some phrases used to talk about learning? Match each verb on the left to a word or phrase on the right.

1. decide to — to ski
2. earn — take lessons
3. brush up on — hitting the ball
4. learn how — a diploma
5. practice — classes
6. take — my skills

B Complete the sentence below with phrases from part A. Change the verb form if necessary.

1. I heard you're interested in playing the violin. Did you
   decide to take lessons ?

2. If you want to get better at tennis, you'll have to .... !

3. I already know how to do karate, but I'm taking lessons just to ....

4. It's hard to learn to dance by myself. I'm going to .... with a friend.

5. Kim graduated from college last May. She .... in engineering.

6. This winter, James wants to ....

30 ▪ Unit 8

3 GUESS THE FACTS

Why do you think tango dancing is so popular? What are some ways people can learn or improve tango dancing?

Watch the video

4 GET THE PICTURE

What reasons do people give for wanting to learn the tango? Check (✓) your answers. Then compare with a partner.

- ☐ They're just interested in dancing.
- ☐ Their friends told them to learn the tango.
- ☐ They want to keep fit and have fun.
- ☐ The tango is exotic and challenging.
- ☐ They didn't like any other dances.
- ☐ The tango has a great rhythm.

5 WATCH FOR DETAILS

How do these people recommend learning or improving tango dancing? Match each person with a recommendation.

.... By starting with group classes or private classes.
.... By practicing with a guy.
.... By going to a tango club.
.... By practicing hard.
.... By taking the initiative and taking a class.

Unit 8 ▪ 31

6 WHAT'S YOUR OPINION?

A How important do you think these qualities are for learning to dance? Rank them from 1 (most important) to 9 (least important).

.... athletic ability   .... curiosity   .... patience
.... competitiveness   .... intelligence   .... self-confidence
.... creativity   .... motivation   .... willpower

B **PAIR WORK** Compare your answers with a partner. Explain how you made your choices. Then talk about these activities. Would your rankings change? Why or why not?

learning a foreign language   learning to play tennis   learning to cook

Follow-up

7 ADVICE TO LEARNERS

A Think of a sport, game, or activity that you have learned. Make a list of different ways to learn it.

Activity ....

Ways to learn
....
....
....
....
....
....
....
....
....
....

B **GROUP WORK** Take turns asking and answering questions about the activities the group members have chosen. Use language like this:

How did you learn to . . . ?   I learned . . . by . . .
Why do you enjoy . . . ?   I enjoy . . . because . . .
What's the best way to learn . . . ?   The best way to learn . . . is by . . .
What's a good way to improve . . . ?   A good way to improve . . . is to . . .

Language close-up

8 WHAT DID THEY SAY?

Watch the video and complete the conversation. Then practice with a partner.

A dance teacher talks about learning the tango.

Kevin: Why do you think tango is so .... ?
Uche: I think tango is .... because it's very ....
and it's also very .... for people, and once
people .... something that they find ....
and it's very ...., I think they ....
very rewarded.
Kevin: What do you .... for people who .... to
learn tango?
Uche: I would recommend starting with .... classes
or .... classes.
Kevin: And .... you've learned the .... of tango,
what's a good way to .... your moves?
Uche: By going out .... with the people that you've ....
the .... with, ... at home, listening to the ....,
just feeling very .... with the music, and then ....
.... dancing again.

9 GERUNDS AND INFINITIVES *Talking about preferences*

A For each pair of expressions, complete the questions.

1. earn a degree / learn for fun
   Would you prefer *to earn a degree or learn for fun* ?
2. learn English in Australia / in Canada
   Would you rather .... ?
3. learn how to cook / how to dance the tango
   Would you prefer .... ?
4. brush up on skills you already have / learn something new
   Would you rather .... ?
5. read English magazines / English novels
   Would you rather .... ?
6. study in the morning / at night
   Would you prefer .... ?

B GROUP WORK Ask several classmates the questions in part A.
Then share their answers with the class.

"Mari would prefer to start a business. Juan would rather learn to dance at home."

This page is intentionally left blank

interchange
FIFTH EDITION

3A

Workbook

Jack C. Richards
with Jonathan Hull and Susan Proctor

CAMBRIDGE
UNIVERSITY PRESS

This page is intentionally left blank

Contents

	Credits	iv
1	That's my kind of friend!	1
2	Working 9 to 5	7
3	Lend a hand.	13
4	What happened?	19
5	Expanding your horizons	25
6	That needs fixing.	31
7	What can we do?	37
8	Never stop learning.	43

Credits

The authors and publishers acknowledge the following sources of copyright material and are grateful for the permissions granted. While every effort has been made, it has not always been possible to identify the sources of all the material used, or to trace all copyright holders. If any omissions are brought to our notice, we will be happy to include the appropriate acknowledgements on reprinting and in the next update to the digital edition, as applicable.

Key: BL = Below Left, BR = Below Right, C = Centre, CL = Centre Left, CR = Centre Right, TC = Top Centre, TL = Top Left, TR = Top Right.

Illustrations

337 Jon (KJA Artists): 51; **Mark Duffin**: 31, 80; **Pablo Gallego** (Beehive Illustration): 10, 20; **Thomas Girard** (Good Illustration): 4, 28, 53; **Dusan Lakicevic** (Beehive Illustration): 1, 14, 22, 33, 96; **Yishan Li** (Advocate Art): 6, 13, 65; **Quino Marin** (The Organisation): 29; **Gavin Reece** (New Division): 3, 64; **Paul Williams** (Sylvie Poggio Artists): 15, 66.

Photos

Back cover (woman with whiteboard): Jenny Acheson/Stockbyte/GettyImages; Back cover (whiteboard): Nemida/GettyImages; Back cover (man using phone): Betsie Van Der Meer/Taxi/GettyImages; Back cover (woman smiling): PeopleImages.com/DigitalVision/GettyImages; Back cover (name tag): Tetra Images/GettyImages; Back cover (handshake): David Lees/Taxi/GettyImages; p. 2 : Michael H/DigitalVision/GettyImages; p. 5 (TL): Jade/Blend Images/Getty Images Plus/GettyImages; p. 5 (TR): Jamie Grill/GettyImages; p. 5 (BL): Blend Images - Jose Luis Pelaez Inc/Brand X Pictures/GettyImages; p. 5 (BR): Tomasz Trojanowski/Hemera/Getty Images Plus/GettyImages; p. 7: John Rowley/Photodisc/GettyImages; p. 8: KidStock/Blend Images/GettyImages; p. 9: monkeybusinessimages/iStock/Getty Images Plus/GettyImages; p. 12 (TL): ColorBlind/The Image Bank/GettyImages; p. 12 (TR): Sigrid Gombert/MITO images/GettyImages; p. 12 (CL): 4x6/E+/GettyImages; p. 12 (CR): Roy Hsu/Photographer's Choice RF/GettyImages; p. 13 (TR): mediaphotos/iStock/Getty Images Plus/GettyImages; p. 16: Purestock/GettyImages; p. 17 : PeopleImages/DigitalVision/GettyImages; p. 18: Phil Boorman/Cultura/GettyImages; p. 19 (TL): Robert George Young/Photographer's Choice/GettyImages; p. 19 (BR): dangdumrong/iStock/Getty Images Plus/GettyImages; p. 21 (TR): Chris Dyball/Innerlight/The Image Bank/GettyImages; p. 21 (CL): MattStansfield/iStock/Getty Images Plus/GettyImages; p. 23: EXTREME-PHOTOGRAPHER/E+/GettyImages; p. 24 (Johnson): George Doyle/Stockbyte/GettyImages; p. 24 (Marshall): Digital Vision./Photodisc/GettyImages; p. 24 (James): Yellow Dog Productions/The Image Bank/GettyImages; p. 24 (Grant): wdstock/iStock/Getty Images Plus/GettyImages; p. 24 (Simpson): Dave and Les Jacobs/Blend Images/GettyImages; p. 25 (TR): asiseeit/iStock/Getty Images Plus/GettyImages; p. 25 (BR): hadynyah/E+/GettyImages; p. 26: Thomas_EyeDesign/Vetta/GettyImages; p. 30: Education Images/Universal Images Group/GettyImages; p. 32 (George): snapphoto/E+/GettyImages; p. 32 (airport): Philippe TURPIN/Photononstop/Photolibrary/GettyImages; p. 32 (Diane): Vesnaandjic/E+/GettyImages; p. 32 (car): lisegagne/E+/GettyImages; p. 34: Whiteway/E+/GettyImages; p. 35 (wrench): TokenPhoto/E+/GettyImages; p. 35 (TR): John E. Kelly/Photodisc/GettyImages; p. 36: pixelfusion3d/iStock/Getty Images Plus/GettyImages; p. 37 (drain): belovodchenko/iStock/Getty Images Plus/GettyImages; p. 37 (plane): incposterco/E+/GettyImages; p. 37 (smoke): Harrison Shull/Aurora/GettyImages; p. 37 (land): Sierralara/RooM/GettyImages; p. 38 (forest): Ro-Ma Stock Photography/Photolibrary/GettyImages; p. 39: Howard Shooter/Dorling Kindersley/GettyImages; p. 40: VCG/Contributor/Visual China Group/GettyImages; p. 41: Travel Ink/Gallo Images/The Image Bank/GettyImages; p. 42: SolStock/iStock/Getty Images Plus/GettyImages; p. 43: Doug Armand/Oxford Scientific/GettyImages; p. 44: Wilfried Krecichwost/DigitalVision/GettyImages; p. 45: cglade/E+/GettyImages; p. 46 (TL): Lew Robertson/StockFood Creative/GettyImages; p. 46 (TC): Alina555/iStock/Getty Images Plus/GettyImages; p. 46 (TR): Jose Luis Pelaez Inc/Blend Images/GettyImages; p. 47 (photo 1): Hemera Technologies/PhotoObjects.net/Getty Images Plus/GettyImages; p. 47 (photo 2): Picturenet/Blend Images/GettyImages; p. 47 (photo 3): Zoran Milich/Photodisc/GettyImages; p.47 (photo 4): DragonImages/iStock/Getty Images Plus/GettyImages; p. 48 (TR): BrianAJackson/iStock/Getty Images Plus/GettyImages; p. 48 (CR): reka prod./Westend61/GettyImages; p. 49 (TR): simazoran/iStock/Getty Images Plus/Getty Image; p. 49 (CR): ONOKY - Eric Audras/Brand X Pictures/GettyImages; p. 49 (BR): michaeljung/iStock/Getty Images Plus/GettyImages; p. 50: leaf/iStock/Getty Images Plus/GettyImages; p. 52 (TL): IP Galanternik D.U./E+/GettyImages; p. 52 (TR): Lady-Photo/iStock/Getty Images Plus/GettyImages; p. 54: Westend61/GettyImages; p. 55 (CR): Andy Sheppard/Redferns/GettyImages; p. 55 (BR): by Roberto Peradotto/Moment/GettyImages; p. 56 (L): Mint/Hindustan Times/GettyImages; p. 56 (R): Michael Runkel/imageBROKER/GettyImages; p. 57: Bettmann/GettyImages; p. 58 (TL): Bettmann/GettyImages; p. 58 (BR): Ron Levine/Photographer's Choice/GettyImages; p. 59: Windsor & Wiehahn/Stone/GettyImages; p. 60: Javier Pierini/Stone/GettyImages; p. 61: blackred/iStock/Getty Images Plus/GettyImages; p. 62: izusek/iStock/Getty Images Plus/GettyImages; p. 63: ADRIAN DENNIS/AFP/GettyImages; p. 67: Greg Vaughn/Perspectives/GettyImages; p. 68: Caiaimage/Robert Daly/GettyImages; p. 69 (TL): marco wong/Moment/GettyImages; p. 69 (TR): Oscar Wong/Moment Open/GettyImages; p. 69 (CL): Otto Stadler/Photographer's Choice/GettyImages; p. 69 (CR): David Hannah/Lonely Planet Images/GettyImages; p. 69 (BL): LOOK Photography/UpperCut Images/GettyImages; p. 69 (BR): lightkey/E+/GettyImages; p. 70: Thomas Kokta/Photographer's Choice RF/GettyImages; p. 71 (Calgary Farmers' Market): Ken Woo/Calgary Farmers' Market; p. 71 (WWF): © naturepl.com/Andy Rouse/WWF; p. 72: Christian Hoehn/Taxi/GettyImages; p. 73 (TL): Rosanna U/Image Source/GettyImages; p. 73 (TC): Mark Weiss/Photodisc/GettyImages; p. 73 (TR): i love images/Cultura/GettyImages; p. 73 (BL): monkeybusinessimages/iStock/Getty Images Plus/GettyImages; p. 73 (BC): Photo and Co/The Image Bank/GettyImages; p. 73 (BR): Alija/E+/GettyImages; p. 74 (stonehenge): Maxine Bolton/EyeEm/GettyImages; p. 74 (people): Peter Dennis/GettyImages; p. 74 (boats): De Agostini/M. Seemuller/De Agostini Picture Library/GettyImages; p. 75 (bigfoot): Big_Ryan/DigitalVision Vectors/GettyImages; p. 75 (footprints): Danita Delimont/Gallo Images/GettyImages; p. 76: Steve Bronstein/Stone/GettyImages; p. 77: kbeis/DigitalVision Vectors/GettyImages; p. 78: mediaphotos/Vetta/GettyImages; p. 79 (T): Oscar Garces/CON/LatinContent Editorial/GettyImages; p. 81: Theo Wargo/Getty Images North America/GettyImages; p. 82 (TL): ColorBlind Images/Blend Images/GettyImages; p. 82 (TR): track5/E+/GettyImages; p. 83: imagenavi/GettyImages; p. 84 (TL): John Wildgoose/Caiaimage/GettyImages; p. 84 (TR): Bloomberg/GettyImages; p. 84 (CL): Chris Ryan/Caiaimage/GettyImages; p. 84 (CR): numbeos/E+/GettyImages; p. 84 (BL): Tom Merton/OJO Images/GettyImages; p. 84 (BR): Ariel Skelley/Blend Images/GettyImages; p. 85 (TL): marcoventuriniautieri/E+/GettyImages; p. 85 (TR): Anadolu Agency/GettyImages; p. 85 (CL): Caspar Benson/GettyImages; p. 85 (CR): Jake Olson Studios Blair Nebraska/Moment/GettyImages; p. 86 (house): Peter Baker/GettyImages; p. 86 (traffic): Levi Bianco/Moment/GettyImages; p. 86 (bike): Billy Hustace/The Image Bank/GettyImages; p. 86 (using mobile): SolStock/E+/GettyImages; p. 87: Image Source/DigitalVision/GettyImages; p. 89: Caiaimage/Paul Bradbury/Riser/GettyImages; p. 90: Dawid Garwol/EyeEm/GettyImages; p. 92: FatCamera/E+/GettyImages; p. 93: c.Zeitgeist/Everett/REX/Shutterstock; p. 94 (TR): shapecharge/E+/GettyImages; p. 94 (BR): borgogniels/iStock/Getty Images Plus/GettyImages; p. 95: Lucidio Studio, Inc./Moment/GettyImages.

1 That's my kind of friend!

1 Complete these descriptions with the words from the list.

1. Eric is so ___modest___! He always has such great ideas and never takes any credit for them.
2. The Wongs like meeting new people and having friends over for dinner. They're one of the most ___outgoing___ couples I know.
3. You can't trust Alice. She always promises to do something, but then she never does it. She's pretty ___unreliable___.
4. James wants to be an actor. It's hard to break into the business, but his family is very ___supportive___ of his dream.
5. I never know how to act around Lisa! One minute she's in a good mood, and the next minute she's in a bad mood. She's so ___temperamental___.

- ✓ modest
- ☐ outgoing
- ☐ supportive
- ☐ temperamental
- ☐ unreliable

2 Opposites

A Complete the chart by forming the opposites of the adjectives in the list. Use *in-* and *un-*. Then check your answers in a dictionary.

- ✓ attractive
- ☐ reasonable
- ✓ helpful
- ☐ flexible
- ✓ dependent
- ✓ competent
- ☐ reliable
- ☐ popular
- ✓ formal
- ☐ experienced
- ☐ cooperative
- ☐ sensitive

Opposites with *in-*		Opposites with *un-*	
incompetent	competent	unattractive	attractive
independent	dependent	unhelpful	helpful
informal	formal	unreliable	reliable

incompetent

B Write four more sentences using any of the words in part A.

1. Alan is very incompetent at work. He makes a lot of mistakes.
2. Jene is very helpful nature girl
3. He is dependent on his parents
4. David is a very sensitive person
5. He is popular in his neibourhood.

3 Add *who* or *that* to the conversation where necessary. Put an *X* where *who* or *that* is not necessary.

A: I'm looking for someone _____X_____ I can go on vacation with.

B: Hmm. So what kind of person are you looking for?

A: I want to travel with someone _____ is easygoing and independent.

B: Right. And you'd probably also like a person _____ is reliable.

A: Yeah, and I want someone _____ I know well.

B: So why don't you ask me?

A: You? I know you too well!

B: Ha! Does that mean you think I'm someone _____ is high-strung, dependent, and unreliable?

A: No! I'm just kidding. You're definitely someone _____ I could go on vacation with. So, . . . what are you doing in June?

4 Complete the sentences with *who* or *that* and your own information or ideas.

1. I generally like to go out with people _who are easygoing and have a sense of humor_.
2. I'd rather travel with someone _____.
3. I don't really want a roommate _____.
4. My classmates and I like teachers _____.
5. My best friend and I want to meet people _____.
6. Most workers would prefer a boss _____.
7. Some people don't like stingy types _____.
8. I don't want to have inflexible friends _____.
9. I feel comfortable discussing my problems with friends _____.
10. My favorite friends are people _____.

5 Two of a kind?

A Read the article. What six personality types are discussed?

DO OPPOSITES ATTRACT EACH OTHER?

Some psychologists believe that we are attracted to people who seem to have the characteristics that we wish we had. For example, if you love music but don't play an instrument, you might be attracted to someone who is a musician. Being with that person allows you to be close to something that is important to you and that you want more of in your life.

Because people are very complex, we can be attracted to several different kinds of people who are our opposites in one way or another. So let's take a look at six principal kinds of characteristics in people, and you can decide which type you are most like and which type is your opposite.

Let's begin with introverted and extroverted people. Introverted people often spend a lot of time inside their minds and can be quiet and reserved. Extroverted people enjoy getting out and spending time with other people. If opposites attract, then there will always be an interest between introverted and extroverted people. Introverted people will get out of their minds and into the world with their extroverted friends or partners, while extroverted people will appreciate the quiet space of the inner world of their introverted friends or partners.

Then there are people who relate to the world from a thinking perspective and others who relate to it from a feeling perspective. Thinkers can be cool and objective in their judgments, while feelers may be warm and passionate about theirs. Because people who spend a lot of time thinking want to feel deeply too, they may be attracted to a feeling kind of person. And someone who is very aware of their own powerful feelings may enjoy the company of a relaxed and logical thinker.

Two other characteristics are those of people who use their five senses to understand the world we live in as opposed to those who use their intuition. Sensing people are very aware of the present moment; they are realistic and practical people. Intuitive people, on the other hand, often spend their time in a future of infinite possibilities where their imagination is as free as a bird. The attraction here could be that intuitive people realize they need the practical know-how of sensing people in order to make their dreams come true. Likewise, the sensors are attracted to the imaginative possibilities they see in intuitive people.

These three different pairs of personality characteristics – the introvert and the extrovert, the thinker and the feeler, and the sensor and the intuitive – are of course found in each individual person. Yet many psychologists believe that a person will more often use one characteristic of each pair, in the same way that people use either their left hand or their right. And, according to the idea that opposites attract, the left hand needs the right hand in the same way that the right hand needs the left!

B Based on the information in the article, what kind of people are you attracted to? Circle the words. Then, using the idea that opposites attract, complete the next sentence with the type of person *you* must be.

1. I am more attracted to a person who is (introverted / extroverted). Therefore, I am _____.

2. I am more attracted to a person who is a (thinker / feeler). Therefore, I am a _____.

3. I am more attracted to a person who is the (sensing type / intuitive type). Therefore, I am a _____.

C Do you agree with the kind of person you seem to be according to part B? Why or why not?

_____

That's my kind of friend! 3

6 Match the clauses in column A with the most suitable clauses in column B.

A	B
1. I like it ___	a. when someone criticizes me in front of other people.
2. I don't mind it ___	b. when people are easygoing and friendly.
3. It upsets me ___	c. when rich people are stingy.
4. It embarrasses me ___	d. when people are a few minutes late for an appointment.

7 Write sentences about these situations. Use the expressions in the box.

I love it . . .   I can't stand it . . .   I don't like it . . .
It upsets me . . .   It bothers me . . .   I don't mind it . . .
I really like it . . .   It makes me happy . . .   It makes me angry . . .

1. I don't like it when people cut in line.

2. _____

3. _____

4. _____

5. _____

6. _____

Unit 1

8 **What are some things you like and don't like about people? Write two sentences about each of the following. Use the ideas in the pictures and your own ideas.**

1. What I really like:

   I love it when someone
   is generous and gives me flowers.
   It makes me happy when

2. What I don't like:

   It bothers me when

3. What doesn't bother me:

   I don't mind it when

4. What upsets me:

   It upsets me when

That's my kind of friend! **5**

9 It really bugs me!

Choose one thing from Exercise 8 that really embarrasses, bothers, or upsets you. Write two paragraphs about it. In the first paragraph, describe the situation. In the second paragraph, say why this situation is difficult for you and describe a situation you would prefer.

> It really embarrasses me when someone is too generous to me. Recently, I dated a guy who was always giving me things. For my birthday, he bought me an expensive necklace, and he treated me to dinner and a movie.
>
> The problem is, I don't have enough money to treat him in the same way. I'd prefer to date someone I have more in common with. In fact, my ideal boyfriend is someone who is sensible and saves his money!

_____
_____
_____
_____
_____
_____
_____

10 Choose the correct word to complete each sentence.

1. I can tell Simon anything, and I know he won't tell anyone else. I can really _____ him. (believe / treat / trust)

2. Kay has a very high opinion of herself. I don't like people who are so _____. (egotistical / temperamental / supportive)

3. It bothers me when people are too serious. I prefer people who are _____ and have a good sense of humor. (easygoing / inflexible / reliable)

4. I like it when someone expresses strong _____. Hearing other people's views can really make you think. (accomplishments / compliments / opinions)

5. Lisa is very rich, but she only spends her money on herself. She's very _____. (generous / modest / stingy)

Unit 1

2 Working 9 to 5

1 What's your job?

A Match the jobs with their definitions.

A/An . . .	is a person who . . . .
1. comedian __f__	a. researches environmentally friendly technologies
2. green researcher ____	b. helps students with their problems
3. guidance counselor ____	c. controls a company's brand online
4. organic food farmer ____	d. creates computer applications
5. social media manager ____	e. grows food without chemicals
6. software developer ____	f. makes people laugh for a living

B Write a definition for each of these jobs: accountant, fashion designer, and flight attendant.

1. _An accountant is someone who_ _____
2. _____
3. _____

2 Challenging or frightening?

A Which words have a positive meaning, and which ones have a negative meaning? Write P or N.

awful __N__   fantastic ____
boring ____   fascinating ____
challenging ____   frightening ____
dangerous ____   interesting ____
difficult ____   rewarding ____

B Write about four more jobs you know. Use the words in part A and gerund phrases.

1. _I think being a comedian would be fascinating._
2. _____
3. _____
4. _____
5. _____

7

3 Career choices

A Match each career and the most appropriate job responsibility.

Careers	Job responsibilities
work for an airline	do research
with computers	teach discipline and fitness
as a high school coach	learn new software programs
be a university professor	work independently
a writer	travel to different countries

B Use the information from part A and gerund phrases to complete this conversation.

Teri: So, what kind of career would you like, Jack?

Jack: Well, I'm not exactly sure. _____Being a writer_____ could be interesting. Maybe blogging about something I'm interested in.

Teri: Hmm. I don't know if I'd like that because I'd have to write every day.

Jack: What do you want to do, then?

Teri: Well, I'm not sure either! I'd love _____. I'd really enjoy being with teenagers all day and _____. On the other hand, I'd be interested in _____.

Jack: Really? What would you like about that?

Teri: Well, I'd love _____ all over the world.

Jack: Oh, I could never do that! I think it would be very tiring work.

C Write a short conversation like the one in part B. Use the remaining information in part A or your own ideas.

A: So, what kind of career would you like?

B: Well, I'm not exactly sure. _____

A: That sounds interesting. But I wouldn't like it because _____

B: What do you want to do then?

A: Well, I'd love _____

B: _____

A: _____

Unit 2

4 What a job!

A Read the magazine interviews. Write the correct job title above each interview. There are two extra jobs.

- ☐ architect
- ☐ freelance artist
- ☐ preschool teacher
- ☐ university professor
- ☐ bus driver
- ☐ house painter
- ☐ train conductor
- ☐ website designer

TELL US ABOUT YOUR JOB

1 _____

I have always enjoyed making things, and what's more interesting than building something that people will use for years? The challenge of discovering exactly how a space needs to be constructed for maximum usefulness and beauty is what makes me wake up with a smile. I often work late at the office, but that's part of the job.

2 _____

Working for yourself is hard because you're responsible for everything. If no one calls you and asks you to work for them, you have to go out and look for work. Luckily, I now have some regular clients. I paint pictures for some expensive hotels. Right now, I'm doing some paintings for the rooms of a new hotel in Hawaii.

3 _____

My friends say my work is less demanding than theirs, but I work just as hard as they do. I spend a lot of time alone because my job can't begin until all the construction work is completed. Usually, the rooms look great when I've finished my work. Sometimes I don't like the colors that customers choose, but I have to do what they want.

4 _____

These days a lot of people are doing what I've been doing for fifteen years. I work closely with my clients to find out exactly what they want to show on the Internet and how to make it look as attractive as possible. My work requires a good eye for art, a command of clear and precise language, and of course, knowledge of the latest technology.

5 _____

I meet all kinds of people: some are the best and others aren't so good. Sometimes I have a great conversation with someone I've never met before. And of course, I have my regulars, people I see every day, and we talk about life. But I always keep my attention on the road.

6 _____

Being with kids all day isn't for everyone, but I love it. I take care of children when their parents are away. I do all kinds of things – I teach, I play games, and I read books. I make sure the children are safe and happy. I have a lot of responsibility, but I love my job. It's very rewarding work even though the pay isn't great.

B Underline the words and phrases that helped you find the answers in part A.

Working 9 to 5

5 First, use words from the list to complete each job title. Then choose the best expressions to compare the jobs in each sentence.

- ☐ assistant   ☐ decorator   ☐ painter   ☐ walker
- ☐ counselor   ☐ instructor   ☐ ranger   ☑ worker

1. A child-care ____worker____ doesn't earn ____as much as____ an accountant.
   - ☑ as much as   ☐ greater than   ☐ worse than
2. A chef's _____ has _____ a waiter.
   - ☐ worse hours than   ☐ not as good hours   ☐ as worse hours as
3. A dog _____ is _____ a student intern.
   - ☐ more interesting than   ☐ not as boring as   ☐ better paid than
4. A house _____ earns _____ a camp counselor.
   - ☐ as bad as   ☐ more than   ☐ not more than
5. A park _____ is _____ a landscaper.
   - ☐ as bad as   ☐ not as well paid as   ☐ worse than
6. Being a yoga _____ is _____ being a professor.
   - ☐ more than   ☐ as much as   ☐ not as difficult as
7. Being an interior _____ is _____ being a sales assistant.
   - ☐ greater than   ☐ earns more than   ☐ more interesting than
8. A guidance _____ has _____ a gardener.
   - ☐ more responsibility than   ☐ not more than   ☐ not as long as

6 Complete these sentences with the correct prepositions. Some of the prepositions may be used more than once. More than one answer may be possible.

- ☐ as
- ☐ at
- ☐ in
- ☐ on
- ☐ with

1. Chonglin works _____ the best Chinese restaurant in Los Angeles.
2. I think working _____ other people is more fun than working alone.
3. I would hate working _____ the media. It would be nerve-racking!
4. Working _____ a dance instructor sounds great.
5. Working _____ an office is less interesting than working _____ a cruise ship.

Unit 2

7 Use the words in parentheses to compare the jobs.

Assistant needed at an outdoor swimming pool. Must be able to swim. Responsible for keeping pool and changing rooms clean. $12/hour. Tues.–Fri. 12–7.

Learn web design! In search of a bright young person to work as an intern for an advertising agency. Some clerical work. $15/hour. Mon.–Fri. 9–5.

1. **A:** An assistant at a swimming pool has shorter hours than an intern.
   (shorter hours)

   B: Yes, but working as an intern is more interesting than being a swimming pool assistant.
   (interesting)

Travel agency needs energetic people. Knowledge of a second language is a plus. Mostly answering the phone. $18/hour. Flexible hours. Five vacation days a year.

Tutors in math, science, English, and music wanted at private summer school. Challenging work with gifted teenagers. Salary negotiable. Mon.–Sat. 3–7.

2. **A:** Working in a _____
   (better benefits)

   B: Yes, but working _____
   (challenging)

Tennis instructor needed at summer camp for 12- and 13-year-olds. Must be excellent tennis player and good with kids. $18/hour. Mon.–Fri. 1–7.

Tour company seeks **guide** to lead bus tours. Great attitude and good speaking voice a must! Fun work, but must be willing to work long hours. $15/hour.

3. **A:** _____
   (make as much money)

   B: _____
   (work longer hours)

City seeks **taxi drivers** for morning shift. No experience necessary; driver's license required. $15/hour plus tips. Mon.–Thu. 7 A.M.–2 P.M.

Office assistant required in small, friendly office. Computer skills an advantage. Interesting work. Some management skills necessary. $20/hour. 6-day week.

4. **A:** _____
   (a shorter work week)

   B: _____
   (less boring)

Working 9 to 5   11

8 Choose four pairs of jobs from the box below to compare. Say which job you would prefer and give two reasons.

- a graphic designer/a TV news director
- an architect/a teacher
- a guidance counselor/a coach
- a doctor/a musician
- a police officer/a politician
- a secret agent/a psychiatrist
- working on a construction site/working in an office
- being self-employed/working for a company

Example: <u>Working as a TV news director sounds more interesting than being a graphic designer.</u>
<u>A TV news director has more responsibility than a graphic designer.</u>
<u>Also, directing the news is better paid.</u>

1.

2.

3.

4.

3 Lend a hand.

1 Would you mind . . . ?

A Complete the request for each situation.

1. You want to borrow a classmate's pen.
   Can I borrow your pen?

2. You want a classmate to give you a ride home after class.
   Would you mind

3. You want to turn down your roommate's TV.
   Is it OK if

4. You want to use a friend's cell phone.
   Do you mind if

5. You want to borrow a friend's car for the weekend.
   I was wondering if

6. You want someone to tell you how to get to the subway.
   Could

B Think of four more things you would need to have done if you were going on a long vacation. Write requests asking a friend to do the things.

1. *Could you water the plants?*
2.
3.
4.
5.

13

2

Accept or decline these requests. For requests you decline, give excuses. Use the expressions in the chart or expressions of your own.

Accepting	Declining
That's OK, I guess.	Sorry, but . . .
I'd be glad to.	I'd like to, but . . .
Fine. No problem.	Unfortunately, . . .

1. **A:** Can I use your computer? My computer crashed.
   B: <u>Sorry, but I'm going to use it myself in a few minutes.</u>

2. **A:** I've just finished this ten-page paper. Could you check it for me, please?
   B: _____

3. **A:** I was wondering if I could stay at your place for a week while my landlord fixes the roof.
   B: _____

4. **A:** Would you mind if I used your cell phone to make a long-distance call to Nigeria?
   B: _____

3

Look at the pictures and write the conversations. Speaker A makes a request. Speaker B declines it. Each speaker should give a reason.

1. **A:** <u>Could you carry these boxes for me? I have a bad back.</u>
   B: <u>Sorry, but I have a bad back, too.</u>

2. **A:** _____
   B: _____

3. **A:** _____
   B: _____

Unit 3

4 Getting what you want

A Scan the magazine article about making requests. What strategies can you use for less formal requests? What strategies can you use for more formal requests?

The Art of Making Requests

When you make a request, it helps to be clear about two things: Firstly, how well do you know the other person? Secondly, how important is it for you to get what you want? Are you willing to take "no" for an answer?

Let's say that you would like to borrow someone's car to go out on Friday night. Because borrowing a car is a big favor, we can assume that you'd probably only ask someone you know well for this favor. In general, when making requests of friends or close acquaintances, you can use a less formal approach.

Now let's imagine that it's very important for you to have that car on Friday night; you have to have it. In that case, you can let the other person know in a less formal, direct way. Here are two possible strategies:

1. Make a statement with *need*: "I need to borrow your car."
2. Use an imperative: "Please lend me your car."

By avoiding questions, this approach makes it more difficult for the other person to say no. If you are willing to put the other person in a possibly awkward situation, then this is definitely the clearest, and perhaps most effective, way of getting what you want.

But maybe you expect the other person to say no, and you can live with that. This attitude allows you to have a cooler, more objective perspective, so you can make your request in a more formal, indirect way.

Here are some examples:

3. Ask about ability: "Could/Can you lend me your car?"
4. Be polite – use *may*: "May I borrow your car?"
5. Ask for permission: "Would it be OK if I borrowed your car?"
6. Express curiosity: "I wonder if I could borrow your car."
7. State the request negatively: "I don't suppose you could lend me your car."
8. Apologize: "I hope you don't mind my asking, but could I borrow your car?"
9. Give a hint: "I have plans for Friday night, but I don't have a car."

This approach gives the other person a polite way to refuse if, for any reason, they don't want to or cannot lend you their car. And even though you know the person well, taking a more formal approach proves to the listener that you realize what a big favor you're asking. It shows them respect and appreciation – which makes it more likely that you'll get the result you want!

B Read the article. Check (✓) if each request is less formal or more formal. Then write the correct number from the article (1–9) for each type of request. Only eight of the numbers will be used.

	Less formal	More formal	Type
1. Close the door.	☐	☐	____
2. It's really cold in here.	☐	☐	____
3. Could you possibly move your car?	☐	☐	____
4. May I borrow your dictionary?	☐	☐	____
5. I was wondering if you could help me with this assignment.	☐	☐	____
6. I need some help moving to my new apartment.	☐	☐	____
7. I'm sorry, but I can't stand loud music.	☐	☐	____
8. I don't suppose I could borrow your camera.	☐	☐	____

Lend a hand.

5 Nouns and verbs

A Complete this chart. Then check your answers in a dictionary.

Noun	Verb	Noun	Verb
apology	*apologize*	invitation	
compliment		permission	
explanation		request	

B Check (✓) the phrase that describes what each person is doing.

1. Don't worry. I know you didn't mean to break it.
   - ☐ returning a favor
   - ☐ accepting an apology

2. I really like your new haircut.
   - ☐ giving a reason
   - ☐ giving a compliment

3. Can I borrow your laptop?
   - ☐ asking for a favor
   - ☐ giving a gift

4. I can't lend you my bike because I need it myself.
   - ☐ declining a request
   - ☐ accepting an invitation

5. Could you help me cook dinner?
   - ☐ making a request
   - ☐ returning a compliment

6 Choose the correct words.

1. My phone didn't work for a week. The phone company _____ an apology and took $20 off my bill. (accepted / denied / offered)

2. A friend of mine really loves to _____ compliments, but he never gives anyone else one. I don't understand why he's like that. (do / owe / receive)

3. Diane is always talking on the phone. She makes a lot of calls, but she rarely _____ mine. Maybe she never listens to her voice mail! (makes / offers / returns)

4. I need to _____ a favor. Could you please give me a ride to school tomorrow? My bike has a flat tire! (ask for / give / turn down)

16 Unit 3

7 Use these messages to complete the phone conversations. Use indirect requests.

Message
For: Silvia
Ms. Karen Landers called. Her flight arrives at 7 P.M. on Tuesday. Please meet her in the International Arrivals area.

Message
For: Mike
Mr. Maxwell called yesterday. The meeting is on Thursday at 10:30 A.M. Don't forget to bring your report.

Message
For: Mark
Ed called this morning. Can he borrow your scanner? If he can, when can he pick it up?

Message
For: Katy
Andy Chow called earlier. Are you going to the conference tomorrow? What time does it start?

---

1. **A:** Is Silvia Vega there, please?
   B: No, she isn't. Would you like to leave a message?
   A: Yes, please. This is Karen Landers calling from Toronto.
   Could you tell her _that my flight arrives at 7 P.M. on Tuesday_ ?
   Would _____ ?
   B: OK, I'll give her the message.

2. **A:** Can I speak to Mark, please?
   B: I'm afraid he's not here. Do you want to leave a message?
   A: Yes, please. This is Ed. Please _____ .
   And if it's OK, could you _____ ?
   B: Sure, I'll leave him the message.

3. **A:** Could I speak to Mike, please?
   B: I'm sorry, but he's not here right now.
   A: Oh, OK. This is Mr. Maxwell. I'd like to leave a message.
   Could _____ ?
   Could _____ ?

4. **A:** I'd like to speak to Katy, please.
   B: She's not here right now. Can I take a message?
   A: Yeah. This is Andy Chow.
   Can _____ ?
   And would _____ ?
   B: OK, I'll give Katy your message.

Lend a hand. **17**

8 Complete the conversation with the information in the box. Add any words necessary and use the correct form of the verbs given.

- ☐ ask Kelly to get some soda
- ☐ borrow some money
- ✓ borrow your wireless speaker
- ☐ bring a big salad
- ☐ buy dessert
- ☐ don't be late

Dan: So, is there anything I can do to help for the party?

Mark: Yeah. I have a list here. Would it be all right _if I borrowed your wireless speaker_? Mine isn't working very well.

Dan: Sure. And I'll bring two extra speakers. We'll have amazing sound.

Mark: Thanks.

Dan: No problem. Now, what about food?

Mark: Well, I thought maybe a salad. Would you mind _____, too?

Dan: Well, OK. And how about drinks?

Mark: Well, could you _____? And please tell her _____. Last time we had a party, she didn't arrive till eleven o'clock, and everyone got really thirsty!

Dan: I remember.

Mark: One more thing – I was wondering if you could _____.

Dan: Um, sure. All right. But, uh, would you mind if I _____ to pay for it?

9 Rewrite these sentences. Find another way to say each sentence using the words given.

1. Can I use your cell phone?
   Would it be OK if I used your cell phone? (OK)

2. Please ask Annie to stop by and talk to me.
   _____ (would)

3. Could I borrow your guitar?
   _____ (wonder)

4. Would you ask Mitch what time he's coming over?
   _____ (could / when)

5. Lend me your hairbrush.
   _____ (mind)

Unit 3

4 What happened?

1 Complete these news stories using the verbs from the box.

1.

- [ ] broke
- [ ] found
- [ ] locking
- [ ] stayed
- [✓] went
- [ ] drank
- [ ] heard
- [ ] shouted
- [ ] waiting
- [ ] wondered

WOMAN TRAPPED IN BATHROOM FOR 20 DAYS

A 69-year-old grandmother in Paris ___went___ to the bathroom – and _____ there for twenty days. What happened? As she was _____ the door, the lock _____. She could not open the door. She _____ for help, but no one _____ her because her bathroom had no windows. After nearly three weeks, the woman's neighbors _____ where she was. Firefighters broke into her apartment and _____ her in a "very weakened" state. While she was _____ to be rescued, she _____ warm water.

2.

- [ ] became
- [ ] checking in
- [ ] entered
- [ ] opened
- [ ] sleeping
- [ ] behaving
- [ ] decided
- [ ] had
- [ ] showed

TIGER CUB FOUND IN LUGGAGE

A woman was _____ strangely when she _____ the Bangkok airport. While she was _____ for an overseas flight, she _____ difficulty with a very large bag. The check-in clerk _____ suspicious and _____ to X-ray the bag. The X-ray _____ an image that looked like an animal. When airport staff _____ the bag, they saw that a baby tiger was _____ under lots of toy tigers. The tiger was taken to a rescue center for wildlife, and the woman was arrested.

2 Join each sentence in column A with an appropriate sentence in column B. Use *as*, *when*, or *while* to join the sentences.

A	B
I was crossing the road.	My racket broke.
I was using my computer.	A car nearly hit me.
We were playing tennis.	The water got cold.
I was taking a shower.	I burned my finger.
I was cooking dinner.	It suddenly stopped working.

1. As I was crossing the road, a car nearly hit me.
2. _____
3. _____
4. _____
5. _____

3 Complete these conversations. Use the simple past or the past continuous of the verbs given.

1. **A:** Guess what happened to me last night! As I __was getting__ (get) into bed, I _____ (hear) a loud noise like a gunshot in the street. Then the phone _____ (ring).

   B: Who was it?

   A: It was Luisa. She always calls me late at night, but this time she had a reason. She _____ (drive) right past my apartment when she _____ (get) a flat tire. It was very late, so while we _____ (change) the tire, I _____ (invite) her to spend the night.

2. **A:** I'm sorry I'm so late, Erin. I was at the dentist.

   B: Don't tell me! While you _____ (sit) in the waiting room, you _____ (meet) someone interesting. I know how you are, Matt!

   A: Well, you're wrong this time. The dentist _____ (clean) my teeth when she suddenly _____ (get) called away for an emergency. So I just sat there waiting for two hours with my mouth hanging open!

20 Unit 4

4 Lost and found

A Read this news story. Who is it about? Where did it take place?

Thank you, Andre Botha!

On December 6, 2015, Andre Botha was in the water, watching the big waves at the Pipeline off the island of Oahu, Hawaii, when he noticed something strange. The two-time world bodyboarding champion realized that professional champion surfer Evan Geiselman was in big trouble. Since the Pipeline has some of the biggest waves in the world and is considered to be the most dangerous place on the planet for surfing, situations like this are, unfortunately, not uncommon.

Botha realized that the surfer, who had entered the inside of a huge wave and was riding it, was knocked off his surfboard when the wave crashed on him. Normally a surfer will come up to the surface of the water a few moments after falling off the board. But there was no sign of Geiselman. Botha began to swim on his bodyboard as fast as he could to where the surfboard was being thrown around by the huge waves. When he reached the surfboard, he saw Geiselman, who looked like he might be dead. The surfer was unconscious and his face was turning blue as Botha tried to bring him back to life in the water. Botha breathed into Geiselman's mouth and hit him on the chest to get him breathing again. Then he began to swim to shore with the surfer's unconscious body. Two lifeguards swam out to meet him, and they brought Geiselman to a hospital.

Surfers and bodyboarders agree that Evan Geiselman would probably not be alive today if Andre Botha had not rescued him. They don't always agree about which sport is best, but surfers and bodyboarders do agree that taking care of each other in the big waves is important. This respect and care for people is a wonderful part of these exciting sports.

Surfing at the Pipeline

Bodyboarding

B Use the article to answer these questions.

1. In what sport is Andre Botha a two-time champion?

2. What sport does Evan Geiselman excel at as a champion?

3. Where is the Pipeline located?

4. What is one way you can help an unconscious person start breathing?

5. Who brought Geiselman to the hospital?

6. What helps make bodyboarding and surfing such wonderful sports?

5
Think of a real or imaginary problem like the one in Exercise 4. Write two paragraphs. In the first paragraph, describe your problem. In the second, say how you solved it.

> A couple of years ago, I got lost in the mountains. I was hiking when it suddenly got foggy. I was really frightened because I couldn't see anything, and it was getting cold. I decided to put up my tent and stay there for the night.
>
> While I was putting up my tent, though, the fog began to clear. . . .

6
Choose the correct verbs to complete the story.

Grammar note: After

In sentences using *after* that show one past event occurring before another, the clause with *after* usually uses the past perfect.
After she **had called** her friend, her cell phone battery died.

Andy and I ____had just gotten____ engaged, so we
(just got / had just gotten)

went to a jewelry store to buy a wedding ring. We _____ a ring when a
(just chose / had just chosen)

masked man _____. After the robber _____ Andy's
(came in / had come in)   (took / had taken)

wallet, he _____ the ring. I _____ it to him when the
(demanded / had demanded)   (just handed / had just handed)

alarm _____ to go off, and the robber _____. We were
(started / had started)   (ran off / had run off)

so relieved! But then the sales assistant _____ us we had to pay for the ring
(told / had told)

because I _____ it to the robber. We _____ her
(gave / had given)   (just told / had just told)

that we wouldn't pay for it when the police _____ and
(arrived / had arrived)

_____ us! What a terrible experience!
(arrested / had arrested)

22 Unit 4

7 What a story!

A Choose the best headline for each of these news stories.

- What a disaster!
- What a triumph!
- What an emergency!
- What a lucky break!
- What a dilemma!

1. _____
Karen Lane was seven months pregnant when she and her husband, Scott, went on vacation to a small **remote** island off the coast of South America. On the first night, Karen was in a lot of pain. There were no doctors on the island, so Scott called a hospital on the **mainland**. They told him they could not send a helicopter because a typhoon was coming. During the night, Karen thought she was going to die. Luckily, the typhoon had passed over the island by the following morning. A helicopter picked Karen up and took her to the hospital – just in time for her to have a beautiful baby girl.

2. _____
Serena Mills was very sick for several months before her final exams this summer. She couldn't study at all. Her parents suggested she should **skip** a year and take the exams the next summer. **Remarkably**, Serena suddenly got well just before the exams, spent two weeks studying, and got the highest grade in her class!

3. _____
Mark Blaine had waited years for a **promotion**. Finally, a week ago, he was offered the position he had always wanted – Regional Manager. On the same day, however, he won $6 million in the lottery. Mark's wife wants him to **resign** from his job and take her on a trip around the world. Mark says he cannot decide what to do.

B Look at the words in bold in the articles. What do you think they mean?

remote _____   skip _____   promotion _____

mainland _____   remarkably _____   resign _____

8 Complete the sentences. Use the simple past, the past continuous, or the past perfect of the verbs given.

1. In 2011, two divers ____discovered____ (discover) the remains of a 200-year-old shipwreck while they _____ (dive) off the coast of Rhode Island, in the eastern United States.

2. After an art show _____ (open) in New York, it was discovered that someone _____ (hang) a famous painting by Henri Matisse upside down.

3. In 2015, workers _____ (find) a chemistry lab from the 1840s while they _____ (repair) a building at the University of Virginia in the United States. The lab was behind a wall of the current building.

4. Chile's Calbuco volcano _____ (surprise) residents of Santiago when it erupted in 2015. Before that, an eruption of Calbuco _____ (not happen) for over 40 years.

What happened? 23

9 Read this situation. Then use the information and clues to complete the chart. Write the name of each reporter and each country. (You will leave one square in the chart blank.)

| Ms. Johnson | Ms. Marshall | Mr. James | Mr. Grant | Mr. Simpson |

Five news reporters – two women and three men – arrived for an international conference on Sunday, Monday, and Tuesday. No more than two people came on the same day. The reporters came from five different countries.

Clues

The women: Ms. Johnson and Ms. Marshall

The men: Mr. James, Mr. Grant, and Mr. Simpson

The countries: Australia, Mexico, Brazil, Singapore, and the United States

The arrivals:

- Mr. Simpson arrived late at night. No one else had arrived that day.
- Ms. Johnson and Mr. Grant arrived on the same day.
- The man who came from Singapore had arrived the day before.
- The reporters who came from Brazil and Australia arrived on the same day.
- Mr. James and the woman who came from Brazil arrived on Tuesday, after Mr. Grant.
- The reporter from Australia arrived the day after the person who came from the United States.
- Mr. Grant came from North America but not the United States.

Reporters' countries and arrival days

Sunday	Name: _____		Name: _____	
	Country: _____		Country: _____	
Monday	Name: _____		Name: _____	
	Country: _____		Country: _____	
Tuesday	Name: _____		Name: _____	
	Country: _____		Country: _____	

5 Expanding your horizons

1 Complete these sentences. Use words from the box.

- ☐ confident
- ☐ depressed
- ☐ fascinated
- ☐ uncomfortable
- ☐ curious
- ☑ embarrassed
- ☐ uncertain
- ☐ worried

1. In my country, people never leave tips. So when I first went abroad, I kept forgetting to tip servers. I felt really _embarrassed_.

2. The first time I traveled abroad, I felt really _____. I was alone, I didn't speak the language, and I didn't make any friends.

3. I just spent a year in France learning to speak French. It was a satisfying experience, and I was _____ by the culture.

4. At first I really didn't like shopping in the open-air markets. I felt _____ because so many people were trying to sell me something at the same time.

5. When I arrived in Lisbon, I was nervous because I couldn't speak any Portuguese. As I began to learn the language, though, I became more _____ about living there.

6. Before I went to Alaska last winter, I was very _____ about the cold. But it wasn't a problem because most buildings there are well heated.

7. When I was traveling in Southeast Asia, I couldn't believe how many different kinds of fruit there were. I was _____ to try all of them, so I ate a lot of fruit!

8. It was our first trip to Latin America, so we were _____ about what to expect. We loved it and hope to return again soon.

25

2 Imagine you are going to travel to a country you have never visited before. Write sentences using the factors and feelings given. Then add another sentence explaining your feelings.

Factors	Feelings
public transportation	anxious (about)
shopping	comfortable (with)
the climate	curious (about)
the food	enthusiastic (about)
the language	fascinated (by)
the money	nervous (about)
the music	uncertain (about)
the people my age	uncomfortable (with)

1. Public transportation is something I'd be anxious about. I'd be afraid of getting lost.
2.
3.
4.
5.
6.
7.
8.
9.

3 Culture shock!

A Make a list of four pieces of advice to help people feel comfortable about traveling abroad.

B Scan the article about cultural differences. Where can you find articles like this? Who was it written for?

Culture Shock

Each society has its own beliefs, attitudes, customs, behaviors, and social habits. These things give people a sense of who they are and how they are supposed to behave.

People become conscious of such rules when they meet people from different cultures. For example, the rules about when to eat vary from culture to culture. Many North Americans and Europeans organize their timetables around three mealtimes a day. In other countries, however, it's not the custom to have strict rules like this – people eat when they want to, and every family has its own timetable.

When people visit or live in a country for the first time, they are often surprised at the differences between this culture and the culture in their own country. For some people, traveling abroad is the thing they enjoy most in life; for others, cultural differences make them feel uncomfortable, frightened, and insecure. This is known as "culture shock."

When you're visiting a foreign country, it is important to understand and appreciate cultural differences. This can help you avoid misunderstandings, develop friendships more easily, and feel more comfortable when traveling or living abroad.

Here are several things to do in order to avoid culture shock.

1. Instead of criticizing, enjoy the new customs you discover each day on your trip as much as possible.

2. If you read or understand the language, read a local newspaper or listen to the radio to find out what news they're likely to be talking about.

3. Talk to people in order to understand their ideas about their own country as well as their thoughts about yours.

4. Remember the proverb, "When in Rome, do as the Romans do." It's a great way to start learning new things!

5. For instance, try one new thing every day, like a food you've never had before, instead of choosing something on the menu that you can have in your own country.

6. Read a book about the history of the place you are in so you will understand it better while you are there.

7. Go to concerts, museums, theatrical performances, and sporting events to appreciate the culture of this country.

8. Remember that traveling is an educational experience, so be ready to question the stereotypes you may have of another country, and learn about the stereotypes people in that country may have about the place you come from.

C Read the article. Use your own words to write definitions for these words.

1. culture _____
2. culture shock _____
3. appreciate _____
4. stereotypes _____

D After reading the article, would you make any changes to the pieces of advice you listed in part A?

4 Complete these sentences by giving information about customs in a country you know.

1. If you go for a long ride in a friend's car, _it's the custom to offer to pay for some of the expenses._
2. When a friend graduates from school or college, _____
_____
3. If you borrow something from a friend, _____
_____
4. When a friend invites you to dinner, _____
_____

5 Contrasting customs

A Read the information about the different customs and find four pairs of countries with contrasting customs. Write the countries on the lines below.

Country	Custom
Brazil	Friends kiss each other three or four times on the cheeks as a greeting.
Denmark	People generally arrive on time for most occasions.
Egypt	People allow their hosts to treat them to meals in restaurants.
France	Service is usually included in the price of a meal in restaurants.
Japan	People bow when they see or meet someone they know.
New Zealand	People usually pay for their own meals in restaurants.
Spain	People usually arrive late for most appointments.
United States	People leave a tip of 15–20 percent in restaurants.

1. _Brazil and Japan_
2. _____
3. _____
4. _____

28   Unit 5

B Read these five cross-cultural situations. Write sentences describing what the visitors did wrong. Use the expressions in the box.

> you're (not) supposed to
> you're (not) expected to
> it's (not) the custom to
> it's (not) acceptable to

1. Enni is from Denmark. When she was on vacation in Spain, some Spanish friends invited her to dinner at 9:00. She arrived at exactly 9:00, but her friends had not even arrived home yet.

   In Spain, you're expected to _____
   _____

2. Kayla is from the United States. During her first week in Paris, she went to a restaurant with some new friends. She was so happy with the service that she left a tip of 20 percent. Her friends were a little embarrassed.

   In France, _____
   _____

3. James is from New Zealand. When he went to Egypt, he was invited to dinner at a restaurant. When the bill came, he offered to pay for his dinner. His Egyptian friend was kind of upset.

   In Egypt, _____
   _____

4. Clara is from Brazil. She was working for a year in Osaka, Japan. One day, when she saw a Japanese co-worker in a bookstore, she went to say hello and kissed him on the cheeks. Her friend was very surprised.

   _____
   _____

5. Brian is from Canada. He was on vacation in Bali, Indonesia, and some new friends invited him to a temple to watch a special dance performance. He arrived on time wearing a clean T-shirt and shorts, but they said he couldn't go inside the temple because he wasn't dressed properly.

   _____
   _____

Expanding your horizons 29

6 Complete these sentences with information about yourself (1–4) and about a country you know well (5–8).

1. One reason I'd feel homesick abroad is _____
2. Something that would fascinate me would be _____
3. Traveling alone is something _____
4. Getting used to hot weather is one thing _____
5. In _____, it's the custom to _____
6. If you have good service in a restaurant, _____
7. You're expected to _____ when _____
8. It's just not acceptable to _____ if _____

7 Write about living in a foreign country. In the first paragraph, write about two things you would enjoy. In the second paragraph, write about two things you might worry about.

> If I lived in Colombia, I'd enjoy learning about the music scene – the local bands and singers who are popular there. Another thing I'd be fascinated by is . . .
> However, one thing that I'd be nervous about is the food. It might be very different from what I know. Something else I might be uncomfortable with is . . .

Unit 5

6 That needs fixing.

1 What's wrong with it?

A What can be wrong with these things? Put these words in the correct categories. (Most words go in more than one category.)

bike   blouse   car   carpet   chair   glasses   plate   sink   tablecloth

chipped	cracked	dented	leaking	scratched	stained	torn

B What is wrong with these things? Use the words in part A to write a sentence about each one.

1. _The car is scratched._   OR
   There's a scratch on the car.

2. _____

3. _____

4. _____

5. _____

6. _____

7. _____

8. _____

9. _____

2 Problems, problems, problems!

A Scan the articles in *Consumer* magazine. Who would read articles like these? Why?

George's Class Trip

George Humphrey is a Spanish teacher at Crockett College in Duluth, Minnesota. Last year, George took his summer class from Duluth to Madrid, Spain. At the end of the six-week trip, George and the twenty students had a delayed flight at the airport in Madrid when they were coming home. Because of the six-hour delay in Madrid, they missed their plane from New York to Minnesota. Everyone had to stay at a hotel in New York City, and they all spent a lot more money than they had expected. They were also more than 24 hours late when they finally got back to Duluth. When George asked the airline office in New York to pay for their hotel and restaurant bills, the airline refused.

George contacted *Consumer* magazine. We talked to a representative of the airline office in Madrid and discovered that, in Europe, airlines must pay for delays – but that does not apply to airlines in the U.S. However, because the delay first occurred in Madrid, George and each student received 400 euros. George was very pleased, especially for his students. In his email to us, George wrote that he believes the law regarding airline delays needs changing in the U.S.

Diane's Vacation

Diane Gleason is a clothing designer in Cincinnati, Ohio. For her vacation last year, she decided to go somewhere she had never been – the southwestern part of the U.S. When she arrived at the airport in Phoenix, Arizona, she rented a beautiful red convertible for her trip. She planned to drive from Phoenix to the Grand Canyon to go hiking with friends for a few days. After she left the airport, Diane spent the night in Phoenix. The next morning, Diane discovered that someone had stolen the car from the parking lot. She called the car-rental agency, and they told her she was responsible for the cost of the car because she had left the keys in it. They would not let her rent another car until she paid for the stolen one. Diane didn't know what to do. She went back to the motel and contacted *Consumer* magazine.

We called the rental agency, and they told us that Diane had not bought special insurance for a stolen car. We told the agency that Diane needed help: she was all alone and feeling worried and depressed about what happened. The agency suggested that we contact Diane's credit card company. We did, and they told us that Diane was protected because of her credit card. They would pay for the stolen car! By evening, Diane had rented another car from the same agency and, that night, she had dinner at the Grand Canyon with her friends.

B Read the articles and complete the chart. Did George and Diane receive money?

	Problems	What *Consumer* magazine did	Received money? Yes No
1. George's trip	delay in Madrid		☐ ☐
2. Diane's vacation			☐ ☐

Unit 6

3   Choose appropriate verbs to complete the sentences. Use passive infinitives (*to be* + past participle) or gerunds.

> **Language note: Verbs ending in -*en* or -*n***
>
> Some verbs are formed by adding -*en* or -*n* to a noun or adjective.
> These verbs mean "to make more of something."
>
> | Noun | Verb | Adjective | Verb |
> |---|---|---|---|
> | length → | length**en** | loose → | loose**n** |
> | (make something longer) | | (make something looser) | |

[✓] lengthen   [ ] loosen   [ ] sharpen   [ ] shorten   [ ] tighten   [ ] widen

1. This jacket is too short.
   It needs to be lengthened.   OR
   It needs lengthening.

2. The screws on these glasses are too loose.
   They need _____

3. The blades on these scissors are too dull.
   They need _____

4. This faucet is too tight.
   It needs _____

5. These pants are too long.
   They need _____

6. This street is too narrow.
   It needs _____

That needs fixing. **33**

4 Complete the conversation. Use *keep*, *keeps*, *need*, or *needs* with passive infinitives or gerunds of the verbs given.

Jack: Guess what? Someone broke into my car last night!

Mia: Oh, no. What did they take?

Jack: Nothing! But they did a lot of damage. The lock _needs to be repaired_ (repair). And the window _____ (replace).

Mia: It was probably some young kids having "fun."

Jack: Yeah, some fun. I think they had a party in my car! The seats _____ (clean).

Mia: How annoying. Does the car drive OK?

Jack: No, it feels strange. The gears _____ (stick), so they _____ (fix). And the brakes _____ (check) right away.

Mia: Well, I guess you're lucky they didn't steal it!

Jack: Yeah, lucky me.

5 Write about something you bought that had something wrong with it. In the first paragraph, describe the problem. In the second paragraph, explain what you did about it.

> Recently, I bought an espresso machine. While I was unpacking it, I could see it was already damaged. The glass carafe was chipped and needed to be replaced. And to make matters worse, the machine leaked!
>
> I took it back to the store. I was worried because the machine had been on sale, and I had lost my receipt. Luckily, the clerk didn't ask me for it. She said a lot of customers had recently had the same problem, and she gave me a better machine at the same price.

Unit 6

6 Paul will fix it!

A Match each problem with the repair needed.

PAUL'S REPAIR SHOP

ITEM	PROBLEM	REPAIR NEEDED
1. dishwasher	doesn't work __f__	a. tighten and glue the legs
2. DVD player	DVD is stuck _____	b. repair the wire
3. speakers	wire is damaged _____	c. remove the DVD
4. dresser	mirror is cracked _____	d. repaint the door
5. stove	metal door is scratched _____	e. replace the mirror
6. table	legs are loose _____	f. check the motor

B Write a sentence describing each problem. Then add a sentence describing the action needed to fix it. Use passive infinitives or gerunds.

1. <u>The dishwasher doesn't work. The motor needs to be checked.</u> OR
   <u>The motor needs checking.</u>

2. _____

3. _____

4. _____

5. _____

6. _____

C Think of three items you own that are damaged (or were damaged) in some way. Write a sentence describing each problem. Then write another sentence describing the action needed to fix it.

1. _____

2. _____

3. _____

That needs fixing. **35**

7 Complete the sentences with the correct forms of the words in the box.

☐ chip	☑ drop	☐ freeze	☐ scratch
☐ clean	☐ fix	☐ jam	☐ stick
☐ die	☐ flicker	☐ leak	☐ torn

1. This cell phone is driving me crazy! My calls keep ___dropping___.
2. Your computer screen is so dirty. It needs to be _____.
3. Something is wrong with your TV screen. It keeps _____. It's time to get a new one.
4. I hate this printer. It keeps _____. The copies won't come out.
5. Be careful – your cup is _____. I don't want you to cut yourself.
6. The buttons on this remote control keep _____. Do you have something to clean it with?
7. Do you realize your jeans are _____ in the back?
8. Your bathroom faucet keeps _____. Do you want me to try to fix it?
9. My new glasses already have a _____ on one of the lenses. How did that happen?
10. Did your laptop _____ again? I find that so annoying.
11. This old scanner doesn't work at all anymore. It needs to be _____.
12. The battery in my cell phone keeps _____. I should buy a new one.

Unit 6

7 What can we do?

1 Use the information in the pamphlet and the verbs and prepositions given below to change the sentences from the active to the passive.

HERE ARE JUST SOME OF THE DANGERS FACING YOU AND YOUR CHILDREN.

The water we drink
1. Agricultural runoff is contaminating the water supply.
2. Chlorine and other additives have ruined the taste of our drinking water.

The food we eat
3. Certain agricultural pesticides have caused new illnesses.
4. Pollution from cars and trucks is destroying our crops.

The air we breathe
5. Factories are releasing dangerous chemicals.
6. Breathing smog every day has damaged many people's health.

The world we live in
7. The lack of rainfall has created more severe droughts.
8. Global warming is threatening our forests and wildlife.

Join **Save Our Planet** today!

1. The water supply is being contaminated due to agricultural runoff. (due to)
2. _____ (by)
3. _____ (by)
4. _____ (because of)
5. _____ (by)
6. _____ (as a result of)
7. _____ (through)
8. _____ (by)

2 Verbs and nouns

A Complete the chart.

Verb	Noun	Verb	Noun
contaminate	contamination	educate	_____
contribute	_____	_____	pollution
_____	creation	populate	_____
deplete	_____	protect	_____
_____	destruction	_____	reduction

B Write four sentences like the ones in Exercise 1 using words from the chart.

Example: <u>Many rivers and streams have been badly contaminated by industrial waste.</u>

1. _____
2. _____
3. _____
4. _____

3 Choose the correct words or phrases.

1. Green organizations are trying to save rain forests that have been __threatened__ by developers and farmers. (created / ruined / threatened)

2. One way to inform the public about factories that pollute the environment is through _____ programs on TV. (agricultural / educational / industrial)

3. In many countries around the world, threatened animal and plant species are being _____ by strict laws. (created / polluted / protected)

4. Agricultural pesticides are _____ the soil in many countries. (damaging / eating up / lowering)

5. _____ is an enormous problem in many large cities where whole families can only afford to live in one room. (pollution / poverty / waste)

El Yunque rain forest

38 Unit 7

4 How safe is the fleece you are wearing?

A Scan the title and first two paragraphs of this article. What is fleece? Do you own clothing made of fleece? What clothing?

The Fleece that Came to Dinner

Today, half of the clothing bought by people is made of a synthetic fiber. And that figure is almost 70% in the developing world. Synthetics – or fibers that are created by science, not by nature – are very attractive to customers because, for example, some of them are water-resistant, which is particularly desirable for rain gear and hiking shoes. Moreover, synthetics don't require the amount of water, labor, and land that is needed to cultivate cotton and other natural fibers.

One of the most popular synthetic fabrics is called fleece, a name that originally referred to the wool from a sheep, which is still used to make fall and winter clothes. But in the twenty-first century, the word "fleece" refers to the inexpensive, lightweight, and often water-resistant synthetic material that more and more people are wearing today.

One of the most interesting things about fleece is the fact that it can be made from recycled plastic bottles. This means that fleece can be far less expensive than wool or other natural fibers. For many people, recycling plastic bottles is thought of as friendly to the natural environment since we are reusing the plastic, not burying it in the ground or dumping it in the oceans. However, in the last few years, scientists have discovered that fleece may not be as environmentally friendly as we once supposed.

Scientists are now finding very small particles of plastic at the bottom of the ocean that they believe are the remains of fleece that is washed in washing machines every day all over the world. When it is washed, more than 1,500 particles may separate from a fleece product into the water. When that water is drained, some of it will make its way back into the lakes, rivers, and oceans of our world. That is what seems to be happening now. When the synthetic particles reach natural bodies of water, the plastic is going to be eaten by fish because it looks like food to them. And sooner or later, those fish are going to be caught, delivered to the food market, and end up on your plate at dinner.

What can be done? Shall we return to more costly, heavier, and traditional natural fibers such as cotton and wool? Are people willing to spend more money to possibly save the environment? Or is economics so important to people who have very little money that they believe they cannot afford to give up their synthetic fibers?

B Read the article. Check (✓) the true statements. For statements that are false, write the true information.

1. ☐ In the developing world, 50% of people buy clothing made of synthetic fiber.

2. ☐ The word "fleece" originally meant sheep's wool.

3. ☐ Fleece is made from recycled plastic bottles.

4. ☐ More than 2,000 particles of fleece may separate during washing.

5. ☐ Fortunately, fish will not consume particles of fleece.

6. ☐ We now know that people are going to stop using fleece because of its dangers.

What can we do?

5 World issues

A Match the nouns and definitions.

Nouns		Definitions
1. infectious diseases	_d_	a. physical actions that are meant to cause destruction or injury
2. global warming	___	b. a period of time when businesses are not doing well and a large number of people cannot find jobs
3. government corruption	___	c. an extreme lack of money
4. famine	___	d. illnesses that can be passed on to other people
5. political unrest	___	e. a situation in which people do not have enough food
6. poverty	___	f. a situation in which citizens become angry or violent due to their dissatisfaction with their government
7. recession	___	g. illegal or dishonest activity by people with political power
8. violence	___	h. a situation in which a number of people are not working because they cannot find jobs
9. unemployment	___	i. an increase in the world's average temperatures

B Choose the correct noun from part A to complete each sentence. You will not use all of the words.

1. It seems like there are more dangerous _____ these days, like swine flu and the Zika virus.

2. During the recent _____, 30 percent of the businesses in my town closed, and a large part of the population didn't have jobs.

3. There's so much _____ in this city. I'm afraid to walk on the streets alone at night because I don't feel safe.

4. Before you travel to a foreign country, make sure there are no dangerous political situations going on there. It can be unsafe to visit countries that are experiencing _____.

5. In the 1800s, a large portion of Irish potato crops were destroyed by disease. Because potatoes were a major part of the Irish diet, there was a major _____ and over 1.5 million people died.

6. People in this country don't trust the police or city officials because there is a lot of _____.

40 Unit 7

6 Complete the conversations. Use the expressions in the box and the information in the list.

> One thing to do . . .
> Another thing to do . . .
> The best way to fight . . .
> One way to help . . .

- [✓] complain to the Parks Department about it
- [ ] create more government-funded jobs
- [ ] create more public housing projects
- [ ] organize a public meeting to protest the threat of public property
- [ ] educate young people about its dangers
- [ ] report it to the local newspaper
- [ ] donate money to charities that provide shelters and food

A new housing development?

1. **A:** A big housing developer wants to build an apartment complex in Forest Hill Park. I think that's terrible, but what can we do?
   B: *One thing to do is to complain to the Parks Department about it.*
   A: That's a good idea.
   B: _____

2. **A:** Personally, I'm worried about violence in the city. The streets are not safe at night.
   B: _____

3. **A:** You know, there's a lot of corruption in our city government.
   B: _____
   A: Yeah, the bad publicity might help to clean things up a bit.

4. **A:** There are so many unemployed people in this city. I just don't know what can be done about it.
   B: _____

5. **A:** What worries me most is the number of homeless people on the streets.
   B: _____
   A: I agree.
   B: _____

What can we do?   41

7 Complete the sentences using the present continuous passive or the present perfect passive. Then suggest a solution to each problem.

1. A lot of jobs ____have been lost____ (lose) in recent years.
   One way to deal with unemployment ____is to bring more businesses____ into the area.

2. These days, a lot of endangered animals _____ (kill) by hunters and poachers.
   The best way to stop this practice _____.

3. During the past few years, lots of trees _____ (destroy) by acid rain.
   One thing to do about it _____.

4. Underground water _____ (contaminate) by agricultural pesticides.
   The best way to deal with the problem _____.

5. Too many people _____ (affect) by infectious diseases in the past few years.
   The best way to stop this _____.

8 Write two paragraphs about a charity, an organization that helps people. In the first paragraph, describe what the charity does. In the second paragraph, explain why you think the charity is useful.

A good charity in my city is Shelter. This organization works to reduce the number of homeless people on our streets. Shelter believes the best way to do this is to . . .

Shelter is my favorite charity because homelessness is, in my opinion, the greatest problem facing my city. Many people cannot find jobs, and . . .

8 Never stop learning.

1 Choose the correct words or phrases.

1. I'm interested in human behavior, so I'm planning to take a class in _____.
(geography / psychology / math)

2. I want to take a course in _____, such as commerce or accounting.
(education / business / social science)

3. I'd prefer not to study _____ because I'm not very comfortable in hospitals. (engineering / new media / nursing)

4. I'd really like to work in Information Technology, so I'm thinking of taking courses in _____.
(computer science / finance / English)

2 What would you prefer?

A Write questions with *would rather* or *would prefer* using the cues.

1. take a science class / an art class

   <u>Would you rather take a science class or an art class?</u>   OR
   <u>Would you prefer to take a science class or an art class?</u>

2. study part time / full time

   _____

3. have a boring job that pays well / an exciting job that pays less

   _____

4. take a long vacation once a year / several short vacations each year

   _____

B Write answers to the questions in part A.

1. _____
2. _____
3. _____
4. _____

3 Love it or leave it

A First, complete speaker A's questions with four things you would not like to do. Use ideas in the box or your own ideas.

> learn to play the accordion
> learn clothing design
> learn how to repair watches
> study sociology
> take a class in personal finance
> take a cooking class

1. **A:** Do you want to learn to play the accordion?
   B: I'd rather not. I'd prefer to learn to play the piano.   OR
   I'd prefer not to. I'd rather learn to play the piano.

2. **A:** Do you want to _____?
   B: _____

3. **A:** Would you like to _____?
   B: _____

4. **A:** Do you want to _____?
   B: _____

5. **A:** Would you like to _____?
   B: _____

B Now write responses for speaker B. Use the short answers *I'd rather not* or *I'd prefer not to* and say what you would prefer to do.

4 Answer these questions and give reasons.

1. On your day off, would you rather stay home or go out?
   I'd rather stay home than go out because _____

2. Would you prefer to have a cat or a bird?
   _____

3. Would you rather live in the city or the country?
   _____

4. When you entertain friends, would you rather invite them over for dinner or take them out to a restaurant?
   _____

5. Would you prefer to see a new movie at the theater or download it and watch it at home?
   _____

5 Online learning, the schools of the future?

A Have you taken an online class? Would you like to? Would you prefer to study online rather than at school? Write your answers.

_____

_____

B Read the online newspaper article. Underline the sentences that contain the answers to these questions.

1. What is a MOOC?
2. Why do so few students complete a MOOC?
3. Do professors who teach MOOCs think that they are as difficult as courses taken in a classroom?
4. What are critics of MOOCs afraid of?

FREE COLLEGE FOR EVERYONE?
posted 21st of August

A revolution in education is going to happen. Massive Online Open Courses (MOOCs for short) are designed for students who cannot afford, cannot get to, or simply don't want to attend classes in a university classroom. MOOCs are going to be of great importance to economically disadvantaged people, as well as people who live far from a university campus. The only requirement to attend a MOOC is access to a computer with an Internet connection, which is becoming more common each day.

Many MOOCs are created by top professors in their fields who teach at prestigious universities in the U.S., like Princeton, Harvard, and Stanford. These professors may teach online courses at their universities, but with a MOOC they can reach students all over the world. At the moment, not all universities accept academic credit for a MOOC. However, almost half of the professors who have taught a MOOC believe that the coursework is as demanding as the work done in a traditional university class. Many of these professors are not paid for teaching MOOCs by their universities; they do it because they want to make education available to everyone, they love teaching, and they enjoy being able to communicate with so many students online.

MOOC students do not pay tuition, which is perhaps the greatest appeal of these courses. Most professors do not even require students to buy textbooks, which can be very expensive as well. This further reduces the cost of education. On the other hand, despite the affordability of MOOCs, MOOC students do not receive diplomas, which may lessen their appeal. Students may receive certification if they pass the course, but of the 33,000 students enrolled in MOOCs today, the completion rate is strikingly low, at only 10%. Because a MOOC doesn't cost anything, students don't have to worry about losing money if they decide to drop the class. And many of them ultimately do.

So while there are upsides to MOOCs, they are not without their critics. Some professors fear that in the future there may be two kinds of university courses: expensive and superior courses at a traditional university where small groups of students meet in classes with their professors, and inexpensive and inferior massive online courses where students will never meet their professors nor even their fellow students. These critics also point out that students must be disciplined self-starters to be successful in a MOOC and that students often develop the skills of perseverance, time-management, and self-discipline by learning together with other students in a traditional university classroom.

C Write answers to these questions.

1. Do you think MOOCs are going to be the courses of the future? Why or why not?

_____

_____

2. What do you see as the main advantage of MOOCs? The main disadvantage?

_____

_____

D What would you prefer to take as a MOOC: a humanities course (such as literature, art, or history) or a science course (such as biology, chemistry, or engineering)? Why did you choose that course?

Never stop learning.

6 Complete the sentences with *by* + gerund. Use *not* if needed. Use the ideas in the box or your own information.

| cook at home | eat out | go out more often | study dance |
| eat good food | exercise regularly | stay home | use social media |

cook at home   *study dance*   *use social media*

1. A good way to enjoy the weekend is not by staying home but by going out with friends.
2. A good way to keep in touch with old friends is _____
3. You can make new friends _____
4. The best way to save money is _____
5. You could stay in shape _____
6. I stay healthy _____
7. One way to learn self-confidence is _____

7 Choose the correct words or phrases.

1. Robin shows her _____ by volunteering to help people with cancer. (competitiveness / communication skills / concern for others)
2. When I was young, I didn't understand the importance of _____. But when I started paying my own bills, I realized it's an important skill. (money management / cooperation / perseverance)
3. I learned _____ from my parents. They taught me the importance of using my imagination and making art. (creativity / courtesy / self-confidence)
4. Gina always gets upset with people who disagree with her. I wish she would show more _____. (perseverance / self-confidence / tolerance)
5. I recently joined a choir, and I love it. But you need a lot of _____, because you have to practice the same piece of music for weeks before you're ready to perform it! (cooperation / perseverance / time management)

8 Personal qualities

A Read about each student in these descriptions and choose a suitable quality for each one.

- ☐ competitiveness
- ☐ creativity
- ☐ self-confidence
- ☐ time management
- ☐ cooperation
- ☐ perseverance
- ☐ self-discipline
- ☐ tolerance

1. Alex is always on time for everything. He's never even five minutes late. He keeps track of everything on his calendar. I wish I were as good at _____ as Alex is.

2. Frank finds school very hard, but no one tries harder than he does. He always spends the whole weekend at the library trying to keep up with his studies. He shows great _____.

3. Melissa always wants to do better than everyone else. In school, she always tries to get the best grades. Her favorite sport is field hockey because she's the best player in the school. No one needs to teach Melissa _____.

4. Jennifer has more _____ than any of her classmates. She writes fascinating stories that show she has a wonderful imagination. She's also very artistic and does very interesting paintings.

B Write two similar descriptions of people you know. Either use two of the qualities you didn't use in part A or choose other qualities.

1. _____

2. _____

Never stop learning. **47**

9 My way

A List two methods of learning each of these skills.

1. become a good guitarist
   - by teaching myself
   - by taking lessons

2. improve my writing ability in English
   - _____
   - _____

3. become a more confident public speaker
   - _____
   - _____

4. learn more about personal finance
   - _____
   - _____

5. become skilled at auto repair
   - _____
   - _____

6. learn a new computer program
   - _____
   - _____

my first guitar

15 years later

B Which of the two methods in part A would you prefer to use to develop each skill? Write sentences using *would rather (not)* or *would prefer (not)*. Give reasons.

1. I'd rather learn guitar by teaching myself than by taking lessons.
   I'd prefer not to take lessons because they're expensive.

2. _____

3. _____

4. _____

5. _____

6. _____

48 Unit 8